Barnfield College Library

T15903

D0247906

AAT

Accounting Systems and Controls

Level 4

Course Book

For assessments from
1 September 2016

First edition June 2016
ISBN 9781 4727 4821 8
ISBN (for internal use only) 9781 4727 4877 5

British Library Cataloguing-in-Publication Data
A catalogue record for this book is available from
the British Library

Published by

BPP Learning Media Ltd
BPP House, Aldine Place
142-144 Uxbridge Road
London W12 8AA

www.bpp.com/learningmedia

Printed in the United Kingdom by Wheatons Exeter Ltd
Hennock Road
Marsh Barton
Exeter
EX2 8RP

Your learning materials, published by BPP Learning Media
Ltd, are printed on paper obtained from traceable
sustainable sources.

All rights reserved. No part of this publication may be
reproduced, stored in a retrieval system or transmitted in any
form or by any means, electronic, mechanical,
photocopying, recording or otherwise, without the prior
written permission of BPP Learning Media.

The contents of this course material are intended as a guide
and not professional advice. Although every effort has been
made to ensure that the contents of this course material are
correct at the time of going to press, BPP Learning Media
makes no warranty that the information in this course
material is accurate or complete and accept no liability for
any loss or damage suffered by any person acting or
refraining from acting as a result of the material in this
course material.

©
BPP Learning Media Ltd
2016

A note about copyright

Dear Customer

What does the little © mean and why does it matter?

Your market-leading BPP books, course materials and e-
learning materials do not write and update themselves.
People write them on their own behalf or as employees of
an organisation that invests in this activity. Copyright law
protects their livelihoods. It does so by creating rights over
the use of the content.

Breach of copyright is a form of theft – as well as being a
criminal offence in some jurisdictions, it is potentially a
serious breach of professional ethics.

With current technology, things might seem a bit hazy but,
basically, without the express permission of BPP Learning
Media:

- Photocopying our materials is a breach of copyright

- Scanning, ripcasting or conversion of our digital
  materials into different file formats, uploading them
  to Facebook or e-mailing them to your friends is a
  breach of copyright

You can, of course, sell your books, in the form in which
you have bought them – once you have finished with
them. (Is this fair to your fellow students? We update for a
reason.) Please note the e-products are sold on a single
user licence basis: we do not supply 'unlock' codes to
people who have bought them secondhand.

And what about outside the UK? BPP Learning Media
strives to make our materials available at prices students
can afford by local printing arrangements, pricing policies
and partnerships which are clearly listed on our website.
A tiny minority ignore this and indulge in criminal activity
by illegally photocopying our material or supporting
organisations that do. If they act illegally and unethically
in one area, can you really trust them?

BPP
LEARNING MEDIA

Contents

Introduction to the course

Syllabus overview

The purpose of the unit is to enable students to demonstrate their understanding of the role of the accounting function in an organisation and the importance of internal controls in minimising the risk of loss. Students will undertake an evaluation of an accounting system to identify weaknesses and assess the impact of those weaknesses on the operation of the organisation.

They will then make recommendations to address the weaknesses having regard for cost/benefit, sustainability and the impact of those recommendations on users of the accounting system. This unit enables students to consolidate and apply the knowledge and understanding gained from the mandatory Level 4 units of *Financial Statements of Limited Companies, Management Accounting: Budgeting* and *Management Accounting: Decision and Control* to the analysis of an accounting system.

When organisations have a planned change in policy there will be a transition period, which will present its own challenges. Students need to be able to review a planned change in policy, identify potential problem areas while one system is being changed to another and make suitable recommendations to ensure that the integrity of the accounting system is maintained.

The accounting system affects all areas of an organisation and should be capable of producing information to assist management with decision making, monitoring and control, as well as producing financial information to meet statutory obligations. In this unit, students will demonstrate analytical and problem-solving skills, exercising judgement to make informed recommendations. These are practical skills that are essential to the accounting technician.

Accounting Systems and Controls requires students to have a sound understanding of management accounting and financial accounting information requirements, and the way that the accounting function needs to support both areas.

Test specification for this unit assessment

This unit is only tested as part of the Level 4 synoptic assessment.

Assessment type	Marking type	Duration of assessment
Computer based synoptic assessment	Partially computer /partially human marked	3 hours

Assessment objectives and Learning outcomes	Weighting
1 Demonstrate an understanding of the roles and responsibilities of the accounting function within an organisation and examine ways of preventing and detecting fraud and systemic weaknesses	10%
Accounting Systems and Controls LO1 Demonstrate an understanding of the role and responsibilities of the accounting function within an organisation LO2 Evaluate internal control systems	

BPP LEARNING MEDIA

Assessment objectives and Learning outcomes	Weighting
2 Evaluate budgetary reporting and its effectiveness in controlling and improving organisational performance **Accounting Systems and Controls** LO1 Demonstrate an understanding of the role and responsibilities of the accounting function within an organisation LO2 Evaluate internal control systems LO3 Evaluate an organisation's accounting system and underpinning procedures **Management Accounting: Budgeting** LO3 Demonstrate how budgeting can improve organisational performance **Management Accounting: Decision and Control** LO1 Analyse a range of costing techniques to support the management accounting function of an organisation LO2 Calculate and use standard costing to improve performance	20%
3 Evaluate an organisation's accounting control systems and procedures **Accounting Systems and Controls** LO2 Evaluate internal control systems LO3 Evaluate an organisation's accounting system and underpinning procedures	15%
4 Analyse an organisation's decision making and control using management accounting tools **Accounting Systems and Controls** LO1 Demonstrate an understanding of the role and responsibilities of the accounting function within an organisation LO2 Evaluate internal control systems LO3 Evaluate an organisation's accounting system and underpinning procedures LO4 Analyse recommendations made to improve an organisation's accounting system **Management Accounting: Decision and Control** LO2 Calculate and use standard costing to improve performance LO4 Use appropriate financial and non-financial performance techniques to aid decision making LO5 Evaluate a range of cost management techniques to enhance value and aid decision making	20%

Assessment objectives and Learning outcomes	Weighting
5 Analyse an organisation's decision making and control using ratio analysis	20%
Accounting Systems and Controls	
LO1 Demonstrate an understanding of the role and responsibilities of the accounting function within an organisation	
LO2 Evaluate internal control systems	
LO4 Analyse recommendations made to improve an organisation's accounting system	
Financial Statements of Limited Companies	
LO1 Demonstrate an understanding of the reporting frameworks and ethical principles that underpin financial reporting	
LO5 Interpret financial statements using ratio analysis	
Management Accounting: Decision and Control	
LO4 Use appropriate financial and non-financial performance techniques to aid decision making	
6 Analyse the internal controls of an organisation and make recommendations	15%
Accounting Systems and Controls	
LO1 Demonstrate an understanding of the role and responsibilities of the accounting function within an organisation	
LO2 Evaluate internal control systems	
LO3 Evaluate an organisation's accounting system and underpinning procedures	
LO4 Analyse recommendations made to improve an organisation's accounting system	
Financial Statements of Limited Companies	
LO1 Demonstrate an understanding of the reporting frameworks and ethical principles that underpin financial reporting	
Management Accounting: Budgeting	
LO3 Demonstrate how budgeting can improve organisational performance	
Management Accounting: Decision and Control	
LO4 Use appropriate financial and non-financial performance techniques to aid decision making	
LO5 Evaluate a range of cost management techniques to enhance value and aid decision making	

BPP
LEARNING MEDIA

Assessment structure

3 hours duration

Competency is 70%

*Note that this is only a guideline as to what might come up. The format and content of each task may vary from what we have listed below.

Your assessment will consist of 6 tasks.

Task	Expected content	Max marks	Unit ref	Study complete
Task 1	Role of accounting function; preventing and detecting fraud and systemic weaknesses	10	Accounting systems and Controls	
Task 2	Effectiveness of budgetary reporting in controlling and improving performance	20	Accounting Systems and Controls Management Accounting: Budgeting Management Accounting: Decision and Control	
Task 3	Accounting control systems and procedures	15	Accounting Systems and Controls	
Task 4	Management accounting tools for decision making and control	20	Accounting Systems and Controls Management Accounting: Decision and Control	

Task	Expected content	Max marks	Unit ref	Study complete
Task 5	Ratio analysis for decision making and control	20	Accounting Systems and Controls Financial Statements of Limited Companies Management Accounting: Decision and Control	
Task 6	Analysis of and recommendations for internal controls	15	Accounting Systems and Controls Financial Statements of Limited Companies Management Accounting: Budgeting Management Accounting: Decision and Control	

BPP LEARNING MEDIA

Skills bank

Our experience of preparing students for this type of assessment suggests that to obtain competency, you will need to develop a number of key skills.

What do I need to know to do well in the Level 4 synoptic assessment?

Accounting Systems and Controls is part of the Level 4 synoptic assessment. This assessment also includes significant elements of the other mandatory units at Level 4 – *Management Accounting: Budgeting, Management Accounting: Decision and Control*, and *Financial Statements of Limited Companies* – for which you should refer to the relevant Course Books, as well as the practice assessments in the Level 4 Synoptic Assessment Question Bank.

To be successful in the assessment you need to:

- Understand the role and responsibilities of the accounting function within an organisation

- Evaluate internal control systems

- Evaluate an organisation's accounting system and underpinning procedures

- Analyse recommendations made to improve an organisation's accounting system

Assumed knowledge

Accounting Systems and Controls is a **mandatory** unit and builds on the fundamental concepts and techniques introduced and developed throughout Levels 2 and 3.

Assessment style

In the synoptic assessment you will complete tasks by:

1 Entering narrative by selecting from drop down menus of narrative options known as **picklists**

2 Using **drag and drop** menus to enter narrative

3 Typing in numbers, known as **gap fill** entry

4 Entering **ticks**

5 Entering **dates** by selecting from a calendar

6 Entering extended **written answers** for human marking.

You must familiarise yourself with the style of the online questions and the AAT software before taking the synoptic assessment. As part of your revision, log in to the **AAT website** and attempt their **online practice assessments**.

Introduction to the assessment

The question practice you do will prepare you for the format of tasks you will see in the Level 4 synoptic assessment.

Information on the scenario for your Level 4 synoptic assessment is issued in advance of the assessment as pre-seen material. You must make sure you are familiar with the relevant pre-seen material before sitting your assessment. Note that the scenario is also included as a pop-up in the live assessment.

It is also useful to familiarise yourself with the other introductory information you **may** be given at the start of the assessment. The following is provided at the beginning of the sample synoptic assessment:

Assessment information

Read the scenario carefully before attempting the questions, you can return to it at any time by clicking on the 'Introduction' button at the bottom of the screen.

Complete all 6 tasks.

Answer the questions in the spaces provided. For tasks requiring extended written answers, the answer box will expand to fit your answer.

You must use a full stop to indicate a decimal point. For example, write 100.57 NOT 100,57 OR 100 57.

Both minus signs and brackets can be used to indicate negative numbers UNLESS task instructions say otherwise.

You may use a comma to indicate a number in the thousands, but you don't have to. For example, 10000 and 10,000 are both okay.

Where the date is relevant, it is given in the task data.

Information

The total time for this paper is 3 hours.

This assessment has a total of 6 tasks which are divided into sub-tasks.

There are 100 marks available in this assessment.

The marks available for each task are shown at the top of each task.

The marks for each sub-task are shown alongside the relevant sub-task.

The data you need to complete each task is contained within that task or through the pop-up windows provided on the task page; you will not need to refer to your answers for previous tasks.

Advice

Read each question carefully before you start to answer it.

Attempt all questions.

You can return to a task at any time during the assessment to check your answers.

BPP
LEARNING MEDIA

1   As you revise, use the **BPP Passcards** to consolidate your knowledge. They are a pocket-sized revision tool, perfect for packing in that last-minute revision.

2   Attempt as many tasks as possible in the **Question Bank**. There are plenty of assessment-style tasks which are excellent preparation for the real synoptic assessment.

3   Always **check** through your own answers as you will in the real assessment, before looking at the solutions in the back of the Question Bank.

Key to icons

Key term
A key definition which is important to be aware of for the assessment

Formula to learn
A formula you will need to learn as it will not be provided in the assessment

Formula provided
A formula which is provided within the assessment and generally available as a pop-up on screen

Activity
An example which allows you to apply your knowledge to the technique covered in the Course Book. The solution is provided at the end of the chapter

Illustration
A worked example which can be used to review and see how an assessment question could be answered

Assessment focus point
A high priority point for the assessment

Open book reference
Where use of an open book will be allowed for the assessment

Real life examples
A practical real life scenario

BPP
LEARNING MEDIA

AAT qualifications

The material in this book may support the following AAT qualifications:

AAT Professional Diploma in Accounting Level 4, AAT Professional Diploma in Accounting at SCQF Level 8 and Certificate: Accounting (Level 5 AATSA).

Supplements

From time to time we may need to publish supplementary materials to one of our titles. This can be for a variety of reasons, from a small change in the AAT unit guidance to new legislation coming into effect between editions.

You should check our supplements page regularly for anything that may affect your learning materials. All supplements are available free of charge on our supplements page on our website at:

www.bpp.com/learning-media/about/students

Improving material and removing errors

There is a constant need to update and enhance our study materials in line with both regulatory changes and new insights into the assessments.

From our team of authors BPP appoints a subject expert to update and improve these materials for each new edition.

Their updated draft is subsequently technically checked by another author and from time to time non-technically checked by a proofreader.

We are very keen to remove as many numerical errors and narrative typos as we can but given the volume of detailed information being changed in a short space of time we know that a few errors will sometimes get through our net.

We apologise in advance for any inconvenience that an error might cause. We continue to look for new ways to improve these study materials and would welcome your suggestions. Please feel free to contact our AAT Head of Programme at nisarahmed@bpp.com if you have any suggestions for us.

Introduction to the organisation

1

Learning outcomes

1.1	**Discuss the purpose, structure and organisation of the accounting function** • Why different types and sizes of organisation, or departments within an organisation, will require different accounting information and systems
1.2	**Discuss the purpose of the key financial reports and their use by a range of stakeholders** • The purpose and content of statutory financial statements • The key external stakeholders of an organisation • How financial information is used by both internal and external stakeholders
1.3	**Examine the impact of relevant regulations affecting the accounting function** • Identify the types of regulations that affect the accounting function

Assessment context

Assessment of these topics will be included within a number of tasks in the synoptic assessment at Level 4.

Qualification context

Statutory financial statements are also covered in the *Financial Statements for Limited Companies* unit at Level 4. Different types of organisation and accounting regulations are covered at an introductory level in *Final Accounts Preparation* at Level 3.

Business context

Understanding the features of different types of organisation, and how these affect both their accounting systems and their reporting requirements, is key to working within accounting functions at higher levels.

Chapter overview

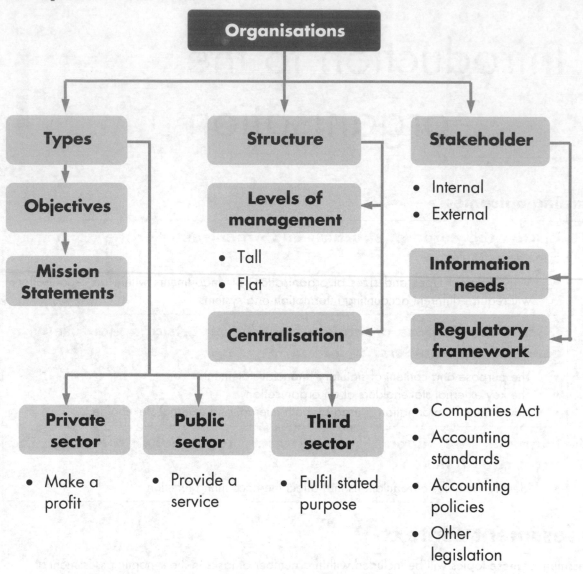

- Internal
- External

Types → **Objectives** → **Mission Statements**

Structure → **Levels of management**
- Tall
- Flat

Centralisation

Stakeholder

Information needs

Regulatory framework

Private sector
- Make a profit

Public sector
- Provide a service

Third sector
- Fulfil stated purpose

- Companies Act
- Accounting standards
- Accounting policies
- Other legislation

BPP
LEARNING MEDIA

Introduction

In this chapter we look at some of the basic principles of the *Accounting Systems and Controls* unit.

We look at various types of organisation and the differences between them, including their **objectives**. We then look at organisation **structure** and its influence over how the organisation operates.

Organisations are also influenced by their **stakeholders** – groups who are in some way affected by the organisation's actions. Stakeholders can be categorised as either internal or external groups, and we look at how the organisation, and its accounting function, must react to the needs of these groups.

Finally we look at the regulatory framework within which the organisation's accounting function exists and the impact this has on it.

1 Organisation types

There are many different types of organisation. You need to be able to recognise why the type of organisation affects how it is structured and how it operates. In turn these factors affect the accounting function, and the accounting and internal control systems, of the organisation.

1.1 Objectives of organisations

The most important way in which organisations differ from each other is by having different objectives. This in turn affects their legal structure and regulation.

Key term

Objective The desired end result.	

Activity 1: Objectives of organisations

Think of a number of organisations that you have dealings with – your employer, your college, a local shop, your local council etc.

Required:

(a) **Identify the objectives of these organisations.**

(b) **In what ways do objectives differ depending on the type of organisation you are considering?**

A business will have a financial objective, which is usually to achieve a level of profit that meets the expectations of its owners.

An organisation that does not exist to make a profit (a not-for-profit organisation or NFP) will usually have the objective of providing the services or performing the other functions that it was formed to do.

1.2 Private sector organisations

Organisations in the private sector comprise:

- Sole traders
- General partnerships
- Limited liability partnerships
- Private limited companies (Ltd)
- Public limited companies (plc)

Sole trader:

- Usually a small business

- Owned and run by just one individual (the proprietor)

- Not a legal entity: no legal distinction between the owner and the business

- Proprietor takes all the profits and suffers all the losses

- Subject to personal tax

- All the assets of the business are owned by the proprietor and all debts of the business are their personal debts so they must pay them from their personal resources

- The proprietor has unlimited liability so that, if the business fails, they are personally liable for all its debts

General partnership:

- The relation which subsists between persons carrying on a business in common with a view of profit

- Usually small to medium-sized businesses (between two and 20 partners)

- Partners are usually fully engaged in management of the business

- Partners personally have unlimited liability for business debts

- Profits are subject to personal tax

- Regulated by Partnership Act 1890

Limited liability partnership (LLP):

- The relation which subsists between persons carrying on a business in common with a view of profit

- Usually medium-sized to large professional firm eg the big accountancy firms

- Partners are usually fully engaged in management of the business

BPP LEARNING MEDIA

- Limited liability for partners – partners are generally not liable for the debts of the business though may lose the money they invested in the business if it fails
- Profits are still subject to personal tax, not business tax
- Must use 'LLP' after its name
- Registered at Companies House
- Regulated by the Limited Liability Partnership Act 2000

Private limited company (Ltd):

- Usually small to medium-sized business though can be very large
- A legal person that exists in its own right
- Company's finances are separate from the owners' personal finances
- Owners are shareholders – individuals or other companies
- Usually shareholders also run the business
- Limited liability for shareholders – they are generally not liable for the debts of the business though may lose the money they invested in the business if it fails
- Must use 'Ltd' after its name
- May not offer shares for sale to the general public
- Registered at Companies House
- Regulated by the Companies Act 2006

Public limited company (plc):

- Usually (but not always) very large business
- A legal person that exists in its own right; finances are separate from the owners' personal finances
- Shares can be traded on a stock exchange
- Usually the majority of shareholders are not involved in running the business
- Run by board of directors, not all of whom are also shareholders
- Limited liability for shareholders
- Must use 'plc' after its name
- Must issue shares to the public of at least £50,000 before it can legally trade
- Can offer shares for sale to the general public if listed on a stock exchange
- Registered at Companies House
- Regulated by the Companies Act 2006
- Listed companies are also regulated by the stock exchange

1.3 Public sector organisations

Organisations include central government, local government and businesses owned by the government.

The objective of public sector organisations is to provide a service rather than sell something at a profit. For example, local government is responsible for many services including:

- Waste collection and disposal
- Street lighting
- Library services
- Museums
- Paths and parks
- Licensing

1.4 The third sector

Some organisations are neither strictly public nor private sector. These include:

- Co-operatives
- Charities

Organisations in this 'third sector':

- Are non-governmental

- Are value-driven

- Reinvest any financial surpluses to advance educational, social, environmental or cultural objectives

Co-operative:

- An organisation owned and controlled equally by the people who use its services or who work in it

- Legal entity

- Shares its earnings with its members as dividends

- Those members are often bound by common social or ethical principles

Charity:

- Has charitable aims, purposes and/or objectives

- Provides a benefit to the public

- Legal entity

- Often run by volunteers

- Has a special tax status

- Must comply with rules and regulations to gain and then retain charitable status

- Registered with the Charity Commission

- Regulated by the Charities Act 2011

Charities can also register as companies, in which case they must also comply with the Companies Act 2006.

The different ways in which organisations are regulated in turn affects their accounting functions and the accounting information they prepare. We shall come back to this later.

1.5 Mission statements

Many organisations seek to summarise their main objective and also their purpose, strategy and values by formulating a **mission statement**.

An organisation's mission includes the following three elements.

Element	Comment
Purpose	Why does the organisation exist and for whom (eg shareholders)?
Strategy	• What do we do? • How do we do it?
Values	What do we believe is important?

Mission statement   A statement of a company's main objective, and its purpose, strategy and values.

Key term

Mission statements are published widely for the benefit of employees and other stakeholders of the organisation. There is no standard format, but mission statements should generally be:

- **Brief**, to help ensure they are easy to understand and remember
- **Flexible**, to help accommodate change
- **Distinctive**, to make the organisation stand out

Illustration 1

The organisation in the scenario for the sample Level 4 synoptic assessment is called SLP Ltd. Its mission statement is as follows:

'We aim to be a market-focused business that specialises in the research, manufacture and distribution of passive electronic components.

Our priorities are quality, service and providing a product range at the cutting edge of technology. We offer our customers cost-effective products of the highest quality.

We aim to develop long-term relationships with all our stakeholders and deal with suppliers, customers and our staff with the highest levels of integrity.'

By calling itself a business SLP emphasises that its primary objective is profitability, but it also refers to the importance of customers, suppliers and employees as stakeholders.

2 Organisation structures

Key term

> **Structure** How activities, functions and staff are grouped, co-ordinated and managed.

Whatever its legal nature (partnership, company or charity), there are many different possible structures for an organisation.

The structure of an organisation affects how it operates and performs.

The most appropriate structure in a given situation depends upon the organisation, its objectives and strategy, the people involved and the nature of its business.

Often structure is determined by the size and age of the organisation rather than by what it needs to be efficient and effective. An inappropriate structure can hinder the success of the organisation.

2.1 Levels of management

A key aspect of organisational structure is how many levels of management there are between the leader of the organisation – the chief executive officer (CEO) or managing director (MD) – and the people actually doing the work.

The structure can be described as either tall or flat.

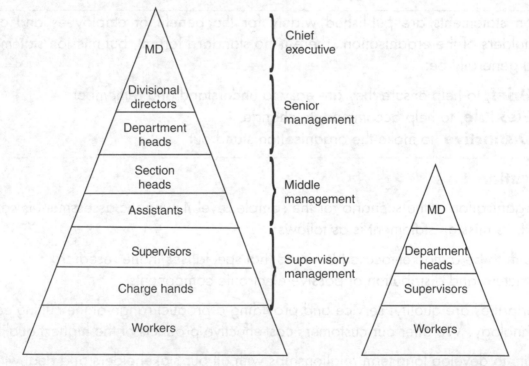

Tall and flat organisations

A **tall** structure:

- Has many levels of management
- Each manager is only responsible for a small number of staff (a narrow span of control)
- Is hierarchical

BPP LEARNING MEDIA

A **flat** structure:

- Has few levels of management from the bottom of the organisation to the top

- Each manager has many staff working for them (this is known as a wide span of control)

The trend in modern organisation structures is to flatten or de-layer, removing whole levels of management.

No one structure is right or wrong; it must fit the organisation type and there are advantages and disadvantages of each.

Activity 2: Tall and flat organisation structures

The NHS is a very large, tall organisation structure with many levels of management.

Idela Snacks is a chain of 3 cafes that is owned and run by only one person, Idela, to whom all 10 staff members are responsible directly.

Required:

(a) What are the advantages of the tall organisation structure for the NHS?

(b) What are the advantages of the flat organisation structure for Idela Snacks?

2.2 Degree of centralisation

Another key aspect of organisational structure is **centralisation**: whether decision-making power and authority are centralised or decentralised.

In centralised organisations:

- Decision-making power and authority are held at one central location, usually a head office function, so people in a department, factory or shop for instance cannot make a decision without consulting head office.

- There is often a tall structure, with decisions being passed up through levels of management to the centre.

- Support functions such as accounting are centralised, and complete tasks for the whole organisation.

- There is close control over all decisions, though the process can become bureaucratic, slow and unwieldy.

Advantages of centralisation:

- Decisions can be co-ordinated more easily, and management have better control over decisions.
- Goal congruence – decisions taken centrally should be based on overall objectives, whereas decentralised decisions may be influenced by short-term or local objectives of the people making the decisions.
- Standardisation – for example, in any country McDonald's customers expect to find standard menus and pricing. If local managers were allowed to take decisions about changing menus or prices, this could undermine the business model.
- Resource allocation – centralised decision-making should allow resource usage to be co-ordinated effectively between different functions and divisions, based on overall corporate objectives.
- Economies of scale – for example, companies might be able to get bulk discounts if they co-ordinate all their purchasing requirements and make a single order. Similarly, the corporate centre may be able to obtain cheaper bank loans and finance than local divisions (which have less assets to secure a loan against).
- Speed of decision-making – for example, when a quick decision is required in response to a crisis, it may not be practical to involve local managers.

In **decentralised** organisations:

- Decision-making power and authority lies with people in each part of the business, perhaps within each operating department, factory, shop etc.
- There is often a flat structure within operating departments, with the leader of each department reporting directly to senior managers at head office.
- There is often a decentralised accounting function, for instance a separate accounting function within each operating department.
- It is much harder to control decisions made by staff.

Advantages of decentralisation:

- Better morale and job satisfaction as local managers are able to take decisions, and this increases their motivation.
- Less pressure and stress on senior managers as they do not have to make all the decisions.
- More experience of decision-making and opportunity for career development for junior managers.
- Local managers may have greater knowledge about operational activities or local market conditions than senior management or head office staff.

BPP
LEARNING MEDIA

- Communication time – although centralisation can be useful for making rapid decisions (eg in a crisis) it may take longer for decisions taken centrally to be communicated to different functions than if the decisions had been taken locally.

3 Stakeholders of organisations

The managers responsible for running a business are not completely free to set objectives; they have different groups of stakeholders to consider.

Stakeholder Individuals or groups that, potentially, have an interest in what the company does

Key term

A stakeholder is anyone who is affected by the actions of the organisation.

Stakeholders can be:

- Internal or external to the organisation
- Directly or indirectly affected by its actions

Activity 3: Internal and external stakeholders

Consider again the NHS and Idela Snacks that you looked at in Activity 2.

Required:

(a) List as many internal stakeholder groups for each organisation as you can.

(b) List as many external stakeholder groups for each organisation as you can.

(c) Consider what information about the organisations each stakeholder may need, and how the accounting function might meet these needs.

Remember not all stakeholders in a stakeholder group will have the same information needs. Try to think about how different groups of employees, for instance, may need to know different things.

3.1 Giving information to stakeholders

Each different type of stakeholder has a different role in relation to the organisation, and therefore different information needs to fulfil that role.

Internal stakeholder	Role	Affected by the organisation's actions	Information needs
Managers	• Allocation of resources to achieve organisation's objectives	Directly	• The objectives of the organisation • The organisation's strategy and detailed plans • Financial information to assess organisation's performance and position – how well its objectives are being met • Management information to make decisions
Employees	• Implementation of strategy, plans and decisions determined by managers	Directly	• Relevant management information to implement decisions
Owners	• Provider of finance • Taker of risk	Directly	• Financial information to assess value of ownership stake and likelihood of financial returns

BPP
LEARNING MEDIA

External stakeholder	Role	Affected by the organisation's actions	Information needs
Bankers	• Provider of finance	Directly	• Financial information to assess organisation's ability to repay loan with interest • May receive some management information on cash flow and profit forecasts
Suppliers	• Provider of goods and services to the organisation	Directly	• Financial information to assess whether organisation will pay its bills
Customers	• User of goods and services provided by the organisation	Directly	• Financial information to assess whether organisation will continue to supply goods and services as required
Government	• Regulator • Manager of infrastructure within which organisation operates • Receiver of tax	Indirectly	• Financial information to assess organisation's liability to tax • Regulatory information to assess organisation's compliance and ability to contribute positively to society (jobs etc)
Community	• Provider of support – or not, depending on stance of organisation!	Indirectly	• Financial information to assess stability

Organisations have to communicate appropriately with stakeholders. The accounting function and accounting systems of the organisation are often the key source of the information they need.

A stakeholder that has a high level of interest in the organisation and also a high level of power – for instance, a bank that has given the organisation a big overdraft – should be regarded as a key player when it comes to giving it the information it

seeks. Many organisations in this position would make sure that it kept the bank well informed and even involved in its decisions.

Other stakeholders, with less of an interest and/or less power over the organisation, should simply be kept informed to the degree required by legislation or contractual requirements.

4 The regulatory framework of accounting

There are many regulations affecting how organisations operate, both within the accounting field and in the wider business environment.

Limited companies are regulated in how they prepare their annual financial statements by:

- **Law** (the Companies Act 2006)
- **Accounting standards** (also called financial reporting standards)

Regulation seeks to ensure that the financial statements of different companies and different types of businesses are as comparable as possible.

Responsibilities in regard to accounting information are spread as follows:

- The accounting function maintains the accounting system and prepares information required of it

- Directors have the statutory duty and responsibility to ensure that 'true and fair' financial statements are prepared

- The external auditor, if there is one, has the statutory responsibility to report an independent opinion on whether the financial statements do in fact give a true and fair view of the company's position and performance

4.1 Companies Act

The Companies Act 2006 sets out the regulatory framework for accounting under which financial statements should be prepared in the UK.

It contains specific requirements about:

- How accounting records should be kept

- What disclosures should be made about, for instance, directors' remuneration

- How annual financial statements should be distributed and filed at Companies House.

The Companies Act 2006 is covered in the *Financial Statements of Limited Companies* unit at this level so no detailed coverage is necessary here.

BPP
LEARNING MEDIA

> **Assessment focus point**
>
> 1 The assessment for this unit is the Level 4 synoptic assessment, in which you will be tested on some of the content of *Financial Statements of Limited Companies* as well as the content of this unit.
>
> 2 If it is some time since you studied *Financial Statements of Limited Companies* you may wish to refresh your memory of the Companies Act now.

4.2 Accounting standards

Accounting standards must also be applied when preparing financial statements for publication.

The aims of these standards are:

- To reduce the variety of methods of dealing with accounting issues

- To increase the comparability of the financial statements of different organisations.

Companies must follow the standards that are relevant to them when preparing financial statements. Because they represent best practice many non-corporate organisations also apply the standards, insofar as they are relevant.

Accounting practice in the UK and elsewhere is increasingly influenced by International Financial Reporting Standards (IFRSs) and International Accounting Standards (IASs), issued by the International Accounting Standards Board (IASB).

> **Assessment focus point**
>
> 1 There are UK standards which, together with the requirements of the Companies Act 2006, form generally accepted accounting practice in the UK (UK GAAP).
>
> 2 You will be assessed however on the international standards, as covered by the *Financial Statements of Limited Companies* unit.
>
> 3 You will also be required to consider how the regulations and standards affect an organisation's accounting function, accounting systems and internal controls.

4.3 Accounting policies

Organisations adopt their own **accounting policies**, which are rules as to how they construct their financial statements. These are discussed in more detail in the next chapter.

4.4 Other legislation

There are other forms of regulation that may impact the accounting function, as a result of either UK Acts of Parliament or EU Directives. These include:

- Taxation regulations including VAT, corporation tax and PAYE for employees

- Data protection law as set out in the Data Protection Act 1998

- Late payment law as set out in the Late Payment of Commercial Debt (Interest) Act 1998

- Money laundering regulations

- Industry regulations – almost every industry has regulations that affect how an organisation operates in that particular industry eg how it disposes of its waste.

BPP
LEARNING MEDIA

Chapter summary

- The objectives of organisations affect their legal structure and regulation.

- The primary objective of a private sector business is to make a profit, while a public sector organisation usually has the primary objective of providing services.

- The legal forms of private sector businesses may be: sole trader; partnership (with unlimited or limited liability for partners); limited liability company (private or public), owned by shareholders.

- The key aspects of a company's structure are: whether it is centralised or not; how many levels of management it has (which determines whether it is a tall or flat structure).

- A company has a range of stakeholders: internal stakeholders (managers, employees and shareholders); external stakeholders (bankers, suppliers, customers, government, the community).

- Stakeholders require information for their various needs and it is the role of the accounting function, and the function of the accounting system, to provide that information.

Keywords

- **Accounting policies:** How the rules set out in company law and accounting standards are applied to the company's particular circumstances.

- **Accounting standards:** Regulations determined externally on how information in a company's financial statements should be presented.

- **Centralisation:** Whether decisions are made by managers at the centre of the company or are devolved to managers within departments.

- **Mission statement:** A statement of a company's main objective, and its purpose, strategy and values.

- **Objective:** The company's desired end result.

- **Stakeholder:** Individuals or groups that, potentially, have an interest in what the company does.

- **Structure:** How activities, functions and staff are grouped, co-ordinated and managed.

BPP
LEARNING MEDIA

Activity answers

Activity 1: Objectives of organisations

(a)   The objectives that are common to most types of organisation:

- Provide goods and/or services
- Operate efficiently
- Keep expenditure and/or revenue within budgets
- Manage cash flow
- Control internal systems effectively
- Manage stakeholder expectations
- Customer satisfaction
- Preserve public reputation

(b)   Differences in objectives – private and public sector organisations:

- Private sector – profit, sales, share price, survival
- Public sector – social/ethical issues, provision of service, equality of access to service

Organisation type affects the organisation's approach to all the factors identified above.

Activity 2: Tall and flat organisation structures

(a)   Advantages of the NHS's tall organisation structure:

- Narrow span of control – easier for management to manage a few employees
- Clear management structure
- Clear lines of responsibilities
- Clear lines of control
- Employees can see a clear progression ladder, which can feel more achievable
- Structure suited for larger organisations

(b)   Advantages of the flat organisation structure for Idela Snacks:

- More freedom and responsibility for employees
- Quicker decision-making by Idela that is not hindered by many levels of management
- Quicker communication from top to bottom
- Less management cost
- Improved team working
- Less bureaucracy

BPP
LEARNING MEDIA

Activity 3: Internal and external stakeholders

(a)   Internal stakeholders for both organisations include:

- Employees
- Management
- Owners

(b)   External stakeholders might include:

- Patients (NHS)
- Community groups
- Customers
- Suppliers
- The Government
- Regulatory bodies
- Society
- Lenders
- Competitors
- Professional associations
- Unions
- Landlords

(c)   Information needs of internal stakeholders might include all financial and management reports (see Chapter 2) plus other *ad hoc* and regular reports that meet the stakeholders' needs.

External stakeholders may wish to have some of the information that internal stakeholders have access to but it would not always be in the organisation's best interest to provide it! Organisations can have different approaches to different external stakeholders – often dependent on their individual power and influence over the organisation. Some information may also need to be provided to meet regulatory requirements, eg tax returns.

Organisations meet the information needs of internal and external stakeholders through effective management information systems (MISs), and this includes accounting systems.

BPP
LEARNING MEDIA

Test your learning

1 **Which of the following is a desirable characteristic of an organisation's mission statement?**

Detailed	
Rigid	
Distinctive	
For internal publication only	

2 **Complete the following statement:**

A company with many layers of management can be described as having a **(1)**_____ organisation structure with managers having a **(2)**_____ span of control.

Picklists:

(1) flat/tall
(2) narrow/wide

3 **Which of the following is an advantage of a decentralised organisation?**

Goal congruence	
Communication time	
Economies of scale	
Standardisation	

4 **Complete the following statement:**

A bank which has lent money to a company is **(1)** _____ stakeholder of the company which is affected **(2)** _____ by the company's actions.

Picklists:

(1) an internal/an external
(2) directly/indirectly

5 **Identify each of the following parties with their responsibility in the context of a company.**

Parties	Responsibility
Directors	Report whether financial statements show a true and fair view
External auditors	Maintain the accounting system
Accounting function	Prepare financial statements for the company

BPP
LEARNING MEDIA

The accounting function

Learning outcomes

1.1	**Discuss the purpose, structure and organisation of the accounting function** • The difference between financial and management accounting • Why different types and sizes of organisation, or departments within an organisation, will require different accounting information and systems • The different accounting team staffing structures that will be required by different types or sizes of organisation
1.2	**Discuss the purpose of the key financial reports and their use by a range of stakeholders** • The purpose and content of statutory financial statements • The purpose and content of financial information produced for internal use • How financial information is used by both internal and external stakeholders **Reports** • Statement of profit or loss • Statement of financial position • Statement of cash flows • Budgetary control reports
1.3	**Examine the impact of relevant regulations affecting the accounting function** • Identify the types of regulations that affect the accounting function • Explain how the structure of the accounting function supports compliance with external regulations • Assess how the existing structure of the accounting function may need to be adapted to comply with changes in external regulations
1.4	**Demonstrate an understanding of the impact of management information requirements on the accounting function** • How organisational requirements will inform the management information system • How management information systems should enable the calculation of performance indicators

Assessment context

Assessment of these topics will be included within a number of tasks in the synoptic assessment at Level 4.

Qualification context

Management accounting has been studied at Level 3 and also in *Management Accounting: Budgeting* and *Management Accounting: Decision and Control* at Level 4. Accounting regulations and the preparation of statutory financial statements have been covered in *Financial Statements of Limited Companies* at Level 4.

Business context

All businesses have some form of accounting function, even if some or all of it is outsourced to external providers. How the accounting function is structured and run, and how it uses the accounting system, is of key importance to the company's success.

BPP
LEARNING MEDIA

Chapter overview

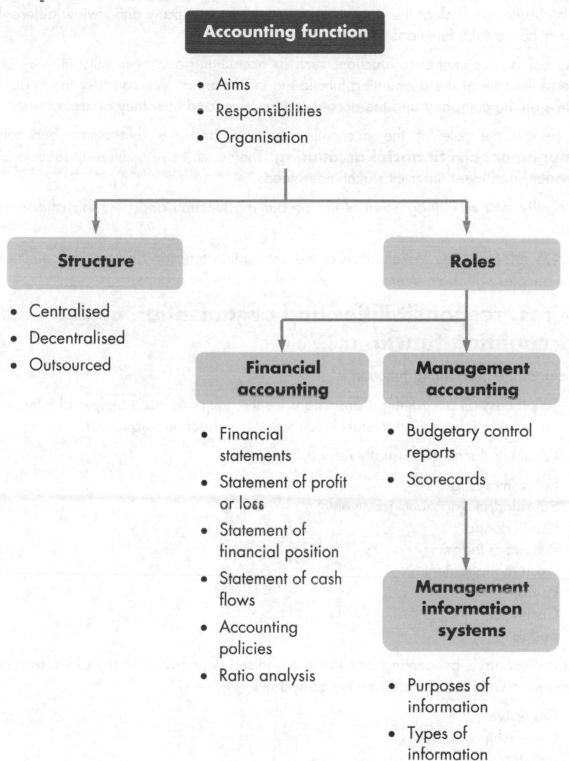

Accounting function

- Aims
- Responsibilities
- Organisation

Structure

- Centralised
- Decentralised
- Outsourced

Roles

Financial accounting

- Financial statements
- Statement of profit or loss
- Statement of financial position
- Statement of cash flows
- Accounting policies
- Ratio analysis

Management accounting

- Budgetary control reports
- Scorecards

Management information systems

- Purposes of information
- Types of information

Introduction

In this chapter we look at the accounting function of a company and review different approaches to such functions in the context of structure.

Many companies centralise functions such as accounting and even outsource all or some of the role of the accounting function to third parties. We consider the impact this has on the company and the accounting function, and how they operate.

We review the role of the accounting function and the differences between **management** and **financial accounting**. They each have a different focus and approach, and meet different stakeholder needs.

We briefly look at management of the accounting function and how this affects its culture.

Finally, we look at key stakeholders of the accounting function and how accounting communicates with both internal and external stakeholder groups.

1 Aims, responsibilities and organisation of the accounting function

The aim of the accounting function is:

- To process all accounting transactions for the company accurately and fully
- To provide information to stakeholders that is correct and up to date

The accounting function is usually responsible for:

- Sales invoicing
- Sales ledger (accounts receivable)
- Credit control
- Purchases ledger
- Cash management
- Payroll
- Costing
- Budgeting

How a company's accounting function is organised depends on many of the factors discussed in Chapter 1, including the company's:

- Objectives
- Ownership
- Stakeholders
- Size
- Age
- Geographical reach
- Industry

These factors also affect the specific tasks the accounting function performs.

BPP
LEARNING MEDIA

Illustration 1

In a partnership the accounting function must maintain capital and current ledger accounts for the partners; these are not necessary in any other type of organisation.

In a manufacturing company the accounting function must establish factory and direct costs, and prepare a manufacturing account; these are not necessary for a service company or a public sector body.

In a large, diverse listed company the accounting function must prepare consolidated financial statements in line with international standards; these are not required in non-companies or in simple companies.

A private sector business selling on credit requires detailed individual accounts for customers; a supermarket making cash sales only does not require this.

In a small accounting function, staff may be organised to perform multiple tasks.

In larger accounting functions for larger companies, there may be clear sections of the function which perform the different responsibilities. There may be separate sections for:

- **Transaction processing** – maintaining the accounting records: payroll, sales ledger, purchases ledger, cash book and general ledger

- **Financial accounting** – producing financial statements and other external reports for regulators, including taxation

- **Management accounting** – producing costing reports, forecasts and budgets, and any other information required by managers to support planning, performance measurement and decision-making

- **Treasury management** – managing the company's cash flows and requirements for finance

2 Structure of the accounting function

In a **centralised accounting function** all accounting tasks are performed at head office, regardless of where the company's other activities are carried out. All departments in the company are served by this one accounting function.

Illustration 2

A large manufacturing company sites the accounting function at head office rather than in the several different locations in which it has manufacturing sites.

Activity 1: Centralised accounting function

Hinton Ltd is a medium-sized company operating on several sites. It has a centralised accounting function.

Required:

(a) **List as many advantages of Hinton Ltd having a centralised accounting function as you can.**

(b) **What do you think are the disadvantages of such an approach?**

Advantages of centralised accounting function:

- Economies of scale as fewer staff overall are needed to complete the same amount of work

- Economies of scope as all departments benefit from having highly trained, expert accounting staff servicing their requirements

- Consistency of approach

Disadvantages of centralised accounting function:

- It is remote from operational centres

- It has little or no direct involvement with the rest of the company

- It may lack relevant expertise if departments are developing innovative business methods

In a decentralised accounting function accounting tasks are performed by separate accounting functions at several different places.

Advantages of decentralised accounting function:

- It may be helpful where the company treats each of its departments etc as a separate profit centre

- It leads to better information flows and communication as the staff are based 'at site'

BPP LEARNING MEDIA

Disadvantages of decentralised accounting function:

- It requires more staff and is therefore more costly

- Accounting staff may lack objectivity as they become too involved in operations

- Accounting staff may miss out on training and development since they become expert only in isolated areas relevant to the operations with which they deal

- Some accounting tasks, such as consolidation for group accounts, require a central approach

Illustration 3

A large manufacturing company has several factories, each with its own accounting function involved in transaction processing and management accounting. A head office accounting function performs the financial accounting and treasury management tasks.

2.1 Outsourcing the accounting function

Many companies centralise some, or more rarely all, of the tasks carried out by an accounting function and then outsource this work to a third party, often under strict service level agreements (SLAs).

Outsourcing of accounting functions is most popular for routine tasks, such as payroll, which:

- Are highly automated
- Rely on information technology for processing
- Require highly specialised and up-to-date skills and knowledge

It is cheaper for small or medium-sized companies to 'buy in' the specialised knowledge from a payroll bureau. This shares skilled staff across several companies, producing economies of scale and a cheaper service for customers.

3 Role of the accounting function

The role of the accounting function is to provide information:

- To internal stakeholders through both financial and management accounting information

- To external stakeholders through financial accounting information (published financial statements)

4 Financial accounting

Financial accounting The process of producing financial statements and other external reports that provide the user with an overview of the financial performance and position of the company.

Key term

Financial accountants summarise financial data from the company's accounting records and present it in the form of reports, including statutory financial statements, which are mainly for use by external stakeholders. The preparation of these is governed by company law and accounting standards, as discussed in Chapter 1.

4.1 Statutory financial statements

Statutory financial statements prepared in accordance with the Companies Act 2006 and accounting standards have the following purposes:

- To determine whether the company has made a profit or a loss

- To demonstrate how well (or otherwise!) the directors have exercised their management or 'stewardship' of the company's resources

- To meet the company's statutory requirement to prepare financial statements that show a true and fair view of its financial performance during a period and its financial position at the end of it

- To help shareholders (and potential new investors) evaluate how far their capital invested in the company is at risk, and determine the return they should be expecting to compensate them for this risk

- To help lenders and suppliers determine whether the company will be able to meet its financial commitments as they fall due

- To help regulators and government determine whether the company is meeting its statutory obligations, eg to submit accurate tax returns, to register the financial statements at Companies House, and to send them to shareholders

- To provide information to other external stakeholders, including competitors and the public at large

The statutory financial statements comprise:

- The **statement of profit or loss**
- The **statement of financial position**
- The **statement of cash flows**

4.2 Statement of profit or loss

> **Statement of profit or loss** A summary of the activity of the company during the reporting period (usually a year).

Key term

It is, in simple terms:

INCOME minus EXPENSES equals PROFIT OR LOSS

The statutory statement of profit or loss for a small company, Arlo Ltd, is laid out as follows.

Arlo Ltd

Statement of profit or loss for the year ending 31 December

	20X1 £	20X2 £
Revenue	40,000	44,000
Cost of sales	(25,000)	(27,200)
Gross profit	15,000	16,800
Administration expenses	(7,500)	(7,700)
Distribution costs	(3,200)	(3,990)
Profit from operations	4,300	5,110
Finance costs	(125)	(130)
Profit before tax	4,175	4,980
Tax	(95)	(140)
Profit for the period	4,080	4,840

In the statutory financial statements of companies some detail on cost of sales and expenses is included as a note to the financial statements rather than on the face of the statement of profit or loss.

4.3 Statement of financial position

Key term

Statement of financial position A list of all of the assets, liabilities and capital of the business at a particular point in time (the end of the reporting period).

It is, in simple terms, the accounting equation:

ASSETS equals CAPITAL plus LIABILITIES

Arlo Ltd
Statement of financial position at the end of 31 December

	20X1 £	20X2 £
ASSETS		
Non-current assets	9,800	10,200
Current assets:		
Inventory	3,050	3,200
Trade receivables	3,600	3,800
Bank	2,570	800
	9,220	7,800
Total assets	19,020	18,000
EQUITY AND LIABILITIES		
Share capital	12,700	12,760
Retained earnings	2,000	840
Total equity	14,700	13,600
Non-current liabilities:		
Loan	1,800	2,000
Current liabilities:		
Trade payables	2,520	2,400
Total liabilities	4,320	4,400
	19,020	18,000

4.4 Statement of cash flows

Statement of cash flows An analysis of why the company's cash balance has changed during a reporting period.

The statement of cash flows separates out the net cash flows during the reporting period arising from:

- Operating activities (net profit for the period plus changes in current assets and liabilities excluding cash)
- Investing activities (buying or disposing of non-current assets)

BPP
LEARNING MEDIA

- Financing activities (paying dividends, taking out or paying back loans, issuing new shares)

The statement of cash flows:

- Explains why the balance of cash at the end of the period is different from the balance at the beginning of the period

- Summarises what the business has spent its cash on in the period

Arlo Ltd

Statement of cash flows for the year ended 31 December 20X2

	£	£
Profit for the period		4,840
Add back:		
Depreciation for 20X2	600	
Increase in inventory	(150)	
Increase in receivables	(200)	
Decrease in payables	(120)	
		130
Net cash from operating activities		4,970
Purchase of non-current assets	(1,200)	
Proceeds from disposal of non-current assets	200	
Net cash from investing activities		(1,000)
Dividend paid	(6,000)	
Proceeds from issue of share	60	
Receipt of loan	200	
		(5,740)
Net change in cash		(1,770)
Cash brought forward		2,570
Cash carried forward		800

4.5 Accounting policies

Financial statements are prepared by the financial accounting section of the accounting function according to rules contained in:

- Company law
- Accounting standards
- The company's **accounting policies**

<table>
<tr><td>Key term</td><td>**Accounting policies** How the rules set out in company law and accounting standards are applied to the company's particular circumstances.</td></tr>
</table>

Illustration 4

Accounting standards require non-current assets to be depreciated. The precise rate at which depreciation is applied is determined by an accounting policy formulated by the company's management.

4.6 Ratio analysis

A key way in which statutory financial statements are used by both internal and external stakeholders is the application of **ratio analysis**.

<table>
<tr><td>Key term</td><td>**Ratio analysis** Making comparisons between figures in a company's financial statements and how they relate to each other in order to determine the performance and position of the company.</td></tr>
</table>

The mechanics of how ratios are calculated are covered in the *Financial Statements of Limited Companies* unit so are not covered in detail here.

Illustration 5

These are the ratios calculated in the Level 4 sample synoptic assessment applied to Arlo Ltd for the periods ended 31 December:

Ratio	Calculation	20X1	20X2	Comments from ratio analysis
Gross profit %	Gross profit/Revenue	37.5%	38.2%	Arlo Ltd has increased its gross margin in 20X2
Operating profit %	Profit from operations/Revenue	10.7%	11.6%	Arlo Ltd has increased its net margin even more in 20X2
Return on capital employed	Profit from operations/(Equity + Non-current liabilities)	26.1%	32.7%	Arlo Ltd has improved its ROCE greatly in 20X2, caused partly by the improved margins but also by decreased capital (most of the retained earnings were returned to shareholders as dividends)

BPP LEARNING MEDIA

Ratio	Calculation	20X1	20X2	Comments from ratio analysis
Gearing	Non-current liabilities/(Equity + Non-current liabilities)	10.9%	12.8%	By increasing its loan and reducing its equity, Arlo Ltd is more highly geared at the end of 20X2
Current ratio	Current assets/Current liabilities	3.7:1	3.25:1	Arlo Ltd is less liquid at the end of 20X2
Acid test or quick ratio	(Current assets less inventories)/Current liabilities	2.4:1	1.9:1	Arlo Ltd is less liquid at the end of 20X2, though not to a worrying degree
Inventory holding period	Inventory/Cost of sales x 365	44 days	43 days	There has been little change in the period
Trade receivables collection period	Trade receivables/Revenue x 365	33 days	31 days	There has been little change in the period
Trade payables payment period	Trade payables/Cost of sales x 365	37 days	32 days	Suppliers are being paid more quickly than before
Working capital cycle	Inventory period + Receivables period – Payables period	40 days	42 days	It took about the same period in both years to convert sales to cash

5 Management accounting

Key term

Management accounting The process of providing internal reports as information for internal stakeholders.

It is not bound by regulation and is intended to meet the needs primarily of the company's management.

Management accounting provides managers with financial information that they can use in order to make critical decisions that affect how the company is run. This includes the preparation of information such as:

- Budgets
- Standard costs
- Variance analysis
- Ratio analysis

- Sales figures for products and or divisions
- Inventory levels
- Profitability reports
- Any other internal information prepared using financial data

These management accounting reports will be used internally by management, to help them:

- Make decisions on resourcing
- Manage the company's profitability and cash flow

5.1 Budgetary control reports

A key report issued by the management accounting function, and assessable in the *Accounting Systems and Controls* unit, is the **budgetary control report**, or variance analysis report.

Key term

Budgetary control report	This compares standard costs and revenues with actual results to obtain variances which explain any deviations and may be used by managers to improve performance.

Illustration 6

Mack Ltd budgeted to make and sell 5,100 units of its sole product in May. Using standard revenues and prices this led to a budgeted profit in May of £30,600. In the end Mack Ltd only produced and sold 4,850 units and only actually made a profit of £24,100.

The budgetary control report analyses how much of the deviation from budget was caused by:

- The change in activity level

- Changes in the price charged to customers and prices paid for materials and labour

- Changes in the efficiency with which materials and labour were used

BPP
LEARNING MEDIA

Mack Ltd
Budgetary control report May 20X2

	£	£	£	
Budgeted profit			30,600	
Sales volume profit variance			1,500	(Adverse)
Standard profit from actual sales			29,100	
	Favourable	Adverse		
Variances				
Sales price		1,400		
Material price		600		
Material usage	500			
Labour rate	200			
Labour efficiency	2,400			
Variable overhead rate		200		
Variable overhead efficiency	510			
Fixed overhead expenditure		4,560		
Fixed overhead volume efficiency	6,290			
Fixed overhead volume capacity		8,140		
	9,900	14,900	5,000	(Adverse)
Actual profit			24,100	

The mechanics of how the standard costs are determined and the variances are calculated are covered in the *Management Accounting: Budgeting* and *Management Accounting: Decision and Control* units, so are not covered here. The management accounting units also cover the meanings of the variances and how they fit together. Understanding and communicating these aspects of the budgetary report are vital roles of the accounting function.

Assessment focus point

1   The assessment for this unit is the Level 4 synoptic assessment, in which you will be tested on some of the content of *Management Accounting: Budgeting* and *Management Accounting: Decision and Control* as well as the content of this unit.

2   If it is some time since you studied you may wish to refresh your memory of variance analysis and budgetary control now.

5.2 Scorecards

Many management accounting functions produce **scorecards** of ratios and other indicators, both financial and non-financial.

The scorecard provides managers with a set of information which addresses all relevant areas of performance in an objective and unbiased fashion.

Scorecards do not only contain indicators which focus on financial performance and position, as ratio analysis does.

Scorecards usually contain measures from at least four different perspectives:

*   Customer satisfaction on issues that matter to customers: cost, quality, delivery, inspection, handling and so on

*   Process efficiency, with the aim of improving internal processes, decision-making and resource utilisation

*   Growth, or the business's capacity to maintain its competitive position through the acquisition of new skills (training) and the development of new products (innovation)

*   Financial success, covering traditional measures such as growth, profitability and shareholder value but directed at what matters to the company's key stakeholders

Targets for these measures are determined by managers, having looked at the company's strategy and how it wants to achieve it.

Important features of the scorecard approach:

*   It looks at both internal and external matters concerning the company
*   It is related to the key elements of a company's strategy
*   Financial and non-financial measures are linked together

Assessment focus point

In the pre-seen scenario material for the sample assessment, based on SL Products Ltd, there is discussion of performance measurement from these four perspectives.

BPP
LEARNING MEDIA

Illustration 7

Here is a scorecard for a restaurant.

Financial Success Customer Satisfaction

Financial success		Customer satisfaction	
Objectives	**Measures**	**Objectives**	**Measures**
To grow and open new restaurants	New restaurants opened	Great service	Excellent results on customer survey
To be profitable	Net profit margins	Repeat business	Customers booking to come again
		Innovative food	New menus on a regular basis
Process efficiency		**Growth**	
Objectives	**Measures**	**Objectives**	**Measures**
TImely food delivery	Time from order to delivery	Trained staff	Employees with relevant training and qualifications
Efficient staff	Processing of food order, few mistakes	New menu choices	Number of new dishes introduced
Low food wastage	Amount of food discarded		

6 Management information systems

Most of the information produced by the accounting function for both internal and external stakeholders is based on data about the transactions that it has processed over a given period. These are recorded in the accounting system, which we shall look at in the next chapter.

Some of the data however comes from the wider management information system, or MIS. This is particularly the case when the accounting function is preparing information for its key internal stakeholder, the management of the company.

6.1 Purposes of management information

All companies require **management information** for a range of purposes:

- Planning
- Controlling
- Performance measurement
- Decision-making

6.1.1 Planning

To plan effectively managers need information that helps them make decisions about what should and can be done:

- The resources that are available
- Timescales
- Likely outcomes under alternative scenarios

6.1.2 Controlling

To control actual performance managers need information to assess whether operations are proceeding as planned or whether there is some unexpected deviation from plan. If so they may need to take some form of corrective action.

6.1.3 Performance measurement

Just as individual operations need to be controlled, so overall performance must be measured and reported, in a budgetary control report or a scorecard.

6.1.4 Decision-making

Good quality information should lead to better informed decisions across the range.

6.2 Types of information

Different types and quantities of information are required by managers for different purposes.

6.2.1 Operational information

Operational information is used to ensure that specific tasks are planned and carried out properly within a factory or office.

Illustration 8

In the payroll section of the accounting function information on the day rates for labour will include the hours worked each week by each employee, the rate of pay per hour, details of deductions and, for the purpose of wages analysis, details of the time each person spent on individual jobs during the week. This information would probably be required weekly. More urgent operational information, such as the amount of raw materials being input to a production process, may be required daily, hourly or, in the case of automated production, second by second.

BPP
LEARNING MEDIA

Operational information is:

- Derived from internal sources
- Detailed, being the processing of raw data
- Relevant to the immediate term
- Task-specific
- Prepared very frequently
- Largely quantitative

6.2.2 Tactical information

Tactical information is used to decide how the resources of the business should be employed, and to monitor how they are being and have been employed.

Tactical information includes:

- Productivity measures (output per labour hour or machine hour)

- Budgetary control or variance analysis reports

- Cash flow forecasts/budgets (not statements of cash flows, which are a form of financial accounting information)

- Efficiency and profitability within a particular department of the company

- Labour turnover statistics within a department

Tactical information is:

- Primarily generated internally (but may have a limited external component)
- Summarised at a lower level
- Relevant to the short and medium term
- Concerned with activities or departments
- Prepared routinely and regularly
- Based on quantitative measures

6.2.3 Strategic information

Managers use **strategic information**:

- To plan the objectives of the company
- To assess whether the objectives are being met in practice

Strategic information includes:

- Overall profitability
- Segmental profitability
- Future market prospects
- Availability and cost of raising new funds
- Total cash needs
- Total resources available
- Capital equipment needs

Strategic information is:

- Derived from both internal and external sources
- Summarised at a high level
- Relevant to the long term
- Concerned with the whole company
- Often prepared on an *ad hoc* basis
- Both quantitative and qualitative
- Uncertain, as the future cannot be predicted

6.3 Information requirements in different sectors

Here are some typical information requirements of a manufacturing company and a service sector company.

Manufacturing company

Information type	Example(s)	General comment
Strategic	Future demand estimates New product development plans Competitor analysis	The information requirements of commercial companies are influenced by the need to make and monitor profit. Information that contributes to the following measures is important: • Changeover times • Number of common parts • Level of product diversity • Product and process quality
Tactical	Variance analysis Departmental accounts Inventory turnover	
Operational	Production reject rate Materials and labour used Inventory levels	

Service sector company

Information type	Example(s)	General comment
Strategic	Forecast sales growth and market share Profitability, capital structure	Companies are customer- and results-oriented. As a consequence, the difference between service and other companies' information requirements has decreased. Businesses have realised that most of their activities can be measured, and many can be measured in similar ways regardless of the business sector.
Tactical	Resource utilisation such as average staff time charged out, number of customers per hairdresser, number of staff per account, customer satisfaction rating	
Operational	Staff timesheets Customer waiting time Individual customer feedback	

BPP
LEARNING MEDIA

In the accounting system:

- The operational level would deal with cash receipts and payments, bank reconciliations and so forth.

- The tactical level would deal with cash flow forecasts and working capital management.

- Strategic level financial issues are likely to be integrated with the company's commercial strategy, but may relate to the most appropriate source of finance.

Chapter summary

- The accounting function aims to process transactions so it can provide information to meet stakeholder needs.

- Sections of a large accounting function are: transaction processing; financial accounting; management accounting; treasury management.

- A major aspect of the accounting function is whether it is centralised, so the same function serves all parts of the company, or decentralised, so different departments etc have their own accounting functions.

- The financial accounting section of the accounting function provides information to both internal and external stakeholders, while the management accounting function meets on the needs of internal stakeholders.

- The company's statutory financial statements serve a number of purposes: to identify profit or loss; to demonstrate the directors' stewardship; to comply with statute; to help shareholders evaluate their investment; to help bankers/suppliers determine the company's ability to pay on time; to help government/regulators determine the company's compliance with is regulatory obligations; to provide information about the company more widely.

- Statutory financial statements comprise statements of: profit or loss; financial position; cash flows.

- Ratio analysis can be applied by both internal and external stakeholders to the information in the financial statements to determine the company's: profitability; liquidity; working capital management.

- The management accounting section provides information to internal stakeholders so they can make decisions on resourcing, and manage the company's profitability and cash flow.

- Key information for managers is found in budgetary control reports to determine why actual performance varies from budgeted performance, and what can be done about it.

- Scorecards of financial as well as non-financial information help the company's managers determine how the company is performing in relation to its: finances; business processes; ability to learn and innovate; customers.

BPP
LEARNING MEDIA

Keywords

- **Accounting policies:** How the rules set out in company law and accounting standards are applied to the company's particular circumstances.

- **Budgetary control report:** This compares standard costs and revenues with actual results to obtain variances which explain any deviations and may be used by managers to improve performance.

- **Centralised accounting function:** All accounting tasks are performed at head office, regardless of where the company's other activities are carried out.

- **Financial accounting:** The process of producing financial statements and other external reports that provide the user with an overview of the financial performance and position of the company.

- **Management accounting:** Producing costing reports, forecasts and budgets, and any other information required by managers to assess whether objectives are being met in practice.

- **Management information:** Information provided to management to help them with planning, controlling, performance measurement and decision-making.

- **Operational information:** Used to ensure that specific tasks are planned and carried out properly within a factory or office.

- **Ratio analysis:** Making comparisons between figures in a company's financial statements and how they relate to each other in order to determine the performance and position of the company.

- **Scorecard:** A set of information which addresses all relevant areas of performance, both financial and non-financial, in an objective and unbiased fashion.

- **Statement of cash flows:** An analysis of why the company's cash balance has changed during a reporting period.

- **Statement of financial position:** A list of all of the assets, liabilities and capital of the business at a particular point in time (the end of the reporting period).

- **Statement of profit or loss:** A summary of the activity of the company during the reporting period (usually a year).

- **Strategic information:** Used to plan the objectives of the company and to assess whether the objectives are being met in practice.

- **Tactical information:** Used to decide how the resources of the business should be employed, and to monitor how they are being and have been employed.

- **Transaction processing:** Maintaining the accounting records: payroll, sales ledger, purchases ledger, cash book and general ledger.

- **Treasury management:** Managing the company's cash flows and requirements for finance.

Activity 1: Centralised accounting function

Advantages of Hinton Ltd's centralised accounting function:

- Greater senior management control of the function's activities

- Standard, consistent procedures

- Decisions can be made taking into account the 'big picture' or the company as a whole

- The company can employ, and benefit from, the skills and experience of more senior, qualified managers and accountants

- In uncertain times the company will benefit from strong, central leadership

- Reporting may be quicker and benefit from standard report layouts and central information

Disadvantages of the centralised accounting function:

- Less decision-making, and therefore less empowerment of junior staff

- Accountants and managers at the central location may lose touch with the operational side of the company, weakening decision-making abilities

- Senior management can be tied up making decisions that should be made lower down the company

BPP
LEARNING MEDIA

Test your learning

1 **Which of the following is the responsibility of the treasury management section of the accounting function?**

Budgetary control reports	
Payroll	
Financial statements	
Cash management	

2 **Which of the following statements about the structure of an accounting function is true?**

A centralised accounting function has better communication with business units than a decentralised one.	
A decentralised accounting function has more economies of scale compared with a centralised one.	
A centralised accounting function has more economies of scope than a decentralised one.	
A decentralised accounting function is better placed to produce group accounts than a centralised one.	

3 **A statement of cash flows shows receipt of a loan as part of _____ and proceeds from the disposal of non-current assets as part of _____.**

Picklist:

financing activities
investing activities
operating activities

4 **Which of the following is the correct expression of the working capital cycle?**

Receivables days + Inventory days – Payables days	
Receivables days + Payables days – Inventory days	
Inventory days + Receivables days + Payables days	
Inventory days – Receivables days – Payables days	

5 The _____ total variance may be analysed into expenditure, efficiency and capacity variances.

Picklist:

fixed overheads
labour
materials
variable overheads

BPP
LEARNING MEDIA

Accounting systems

3

Learning outcomes

1.1	**Discuss the purpose, structure and organisation of the accounting function**
	• The importance of accuracy and cost-effectiveness within the accounting system
	• The importance of ethics and sustainability within the accounting function
1.2	**Discuss the purpose of the key financial reports and their use by a range of stakeholders**
	• The importance of ethical information and sustainability practices to internal and external stakeholders
3.1	**Examine an organisation's accounting system and its effectiveness**
	• Identify the varying financial information requirements of stakeholders (payroll, sales accounting, purchases accounting, general ledger, cash-book and costing systems)
	• Explain how a fully integrated accounting system enables the extraction of information to meet internal and external reporting and monitoring requirements
	• Identify how an organisation's accounting system can support ethical standards and sustainability practices
	• Identify weaknesses in accounting systems that impact on cost-effectiveness, reliability and timeliness
	• Evaluate impact of weaknesses in an accounting system in terms of time, money and reputation
3.2	**Evaluate the underpinning procedures of an accounting system, assessing the impact on the operation of the organisation**
	• Identify how underpinning procedures in the organisation impact on the operation of the organisation (payroll, authorisation and control of sales, purchases, capital expenditure, overheads, payments and receipts)
	• Identify how underpinning procedures in the organisation can support ethical standards and sustainability practices
	• Identify weaknesses in the underpinning procedures and the impact on cost-effectiveness, reliability and timeliness
	• Evaluate the impact of weaknesses in the underpinning procedures in terms of time, money and reputation

3.4	**Examine current and planned methods of operating**
	• Explain why accounting systems should be reviewed regularly to ensure they are fit for purpose
	• Identify and review the methods of operating used by an organisation to ensure that they:
	– are cost-effective
	– encourage ethical standards
	– support sustainability principles and practices
	• Evaluate a computerised accounting system's suitability for the specific information needs of the organisation
4.1	**Identify changes to the accounting system or parts of the accounting system**
	• Identify suitable changes to the accounting system
	• Explain any assumptions made
4.2	**Analyse the implications of changes to the accounting system**
	• Evaluate the implications of the changes to operating procedures and time spent
	• Review recommendations against ethical and sustainability principles, including social, corporate and environmental issues
	• Undertake a SWOT analysis
4.3	**Consider the effects of recommended changes on users of the system**
	• Identify the changes that users may be required to make to working practices to comply with changes to statutory and organisational requirements
	• Consider different methods of support that can be given to users of the accounting system to assist them in adapting to the recommended changes

Assessment context

Assessment of these topics will be included within a number of tasks in the synoptic assessment at Level 4.

Qualification context

How the accounting system works, especially the bookkeeping system, is covered at earlier stages of your studies in Level 2 and Level 3, as are the topics of ethics and sustainability.

Business context

The accounting system is operated by the accounting function to produce information for both internal and external stakeholders. Its efficient and cost-effective operation is key to the company's success.

BPP
LEARNING MEDIA

Chapter overview

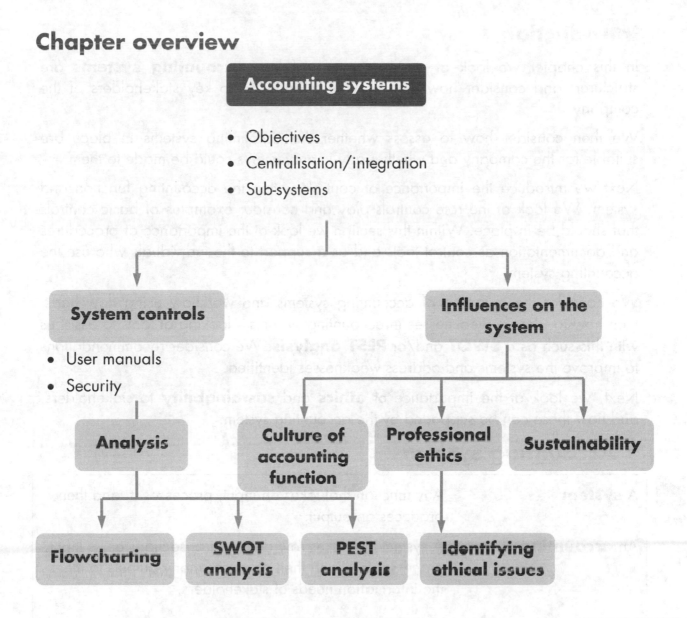

Accounting systems

- Objectives
- Centralisation/integration
- Sub-systems

System controls

- User manuals
- Security

Influences on the system

Analysis

Culture of accounting function

Professional ethics

Sustainability

Flowcharting

SWOT analysis

PEST analysis

Identifying ethical issues

Introduction

In this chapter we look at some examples of how **accounting systems** are structured and consider how they provide information to key stakeholders of the company.

We then consider how to assess whether the accounting systems in place are suitable for the company and whether any improvements could be made to them.

Next we introduce the importance of controls within the accounting function and system. We look at the role controls play and consider examples of basic controls that should be in place. Within this section we look at the importance of procedures and documentation as control tools and as a support to the individuals who use the accounting system.

We consider the mapping of accounting systems and workflow using flowcharts, then how to identify weaknesses in accounting systems – looking at tools to assist us with this such as a **SWOT** and/or **PEST analysis**. We consider recommendations to improve the systems and address weaknesses identified.

Next, we look at the importance of **ethics** and **sustainability** to stakeholders, and how these can be supported by the accounting system.

1 Accounting systems

Key term

A **system**	Any function that takes an input, processes it, and then produces an output.
An **accounting system**	A system that takes raw data on transactions as its input, processes this, and then produces many outputs to meet the information needs of stakeholders.

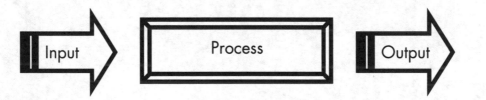

1.1 Objectives of the accounting system

An accounting **system** is effective if it meets the following objectives:

- Operates effectively – processing all transactions accurately and fully

- Reports accurately – providing financial and management information to stakeholders that is cost-effective, reliable and timely

- Complies with applicable laws and regulations

An accounting system that fails to achieve these objectives produces information that:

- Is more expensive to produce than the value gained from it (cost exceeds benefit)

BPP
LEARNING MEDIA

- Is inaccurate and incomplete
- Is unavailable at the time required when key decisions need to be made
- Fails to comply with applicable laws and regulations

1.2 Centralisation of the accounting system

Accounting systems within companies can be centralised (integrated) or decentralised.

- In a centralised, **integrated accounting system** all the data is stored at a central location and accounting function staff process it centrally, although this may be by accessing the system from many different locations.

- In a decentralised accounting system the data is stored and processed separately, perhaps independently by staff at different locations or with different computers. There is no link between processes, each being formed independently of the others.

Activity 1: Centralisation of the accounting system

Read through the CCC scenario at the end of this Course Book (it is quite long, but we will be referring to it often so it is worth taking the time to read it properly).

Required:

(a) **What are the advantages for CCC of a centralised, integrated accounting system?**

(b) **What advantages would a decentralised, integrated accounting system have for CCC?**

(c) **Would a centralised or decentralised accounting system be more appropriate for CCC?**

1.3 Sub-systems of the accounting system

Sub-systems within the accounting system include:

- Payroll
- Recording sales
- Recording purchases
- Paying suppliers
- Recording and banking receipts from customers
- Recording and managing petty cash
- Maintaining the general ledger
- Maintaining the cash book
- Recording time worked on clients/jobs
- Recording materials used on clients/jobs
- Calculating standard costs

2 Accounting system controls

All systems in the company must be controlled so that they operate efficiently and effectively. Any potential weaknesses in the system, or **systemic weaknesses**, need to be addressed by controls.

The accounting system must have built-in controls so that it meets:

- Regulations
- The rules and procedures of the company
- The information requirements of internal and external stakeholders

System controls can include:

- Computer controls (such as passwords or restrictions on staff performing certain operations)

- Manual controls (such as internal audit reviews and supervisory checks)

We look at specific examples of internal controls in the accounting system in Chapter 4.

2.1 User manuals

Accounting system controls need to be kept under review to ensure they are appropriate and effective, so that the information output from the system is on time and of the correct quality.

To enable this, the accounting function should maintain an accurate **user manual** of how the accounting system, and its controls, operate.

BPP
LEARNING MEDIA

Activity 2: Documentation of controls

Hinton Ltd, a medium-sized company operating on several sites, has developed a full user manual for its accounting system.

(a) **What are the advantages of the accounting system having a full user manual for all activities that take place within it?**

(b) **What might the disadvantages of such an approach be?**

2.2 Security of the accounting system

The **integrity** of the accounting system must be secured so that it can perform its function. Threats to system security include:

- Error:
    - Entering transactions inaccurately
    - Failure to detect or correct errors
    - Processing the wrong files

- Data loss caused by:
    - Hardware and software errors
    - Disasters (fire, flood etc)
    - Access by unauthorised persons

- Malicious damage

- Fraud

To ensure security, managers should focus on implementing controls that:

- Prevent threats as far as possible

- Avoid the consequences of threats eg by changing the design of the system and its controls

- Detect errors, bad practice etc

- Plan for recovery procedures eg accessing backups and having a system off site that can be used quickly

There are three types of **security control**:

- Integrity controls to verify and validate input data, the processing of data and the production of reports

- System controls eg anti-fraud and error controls, backup and archiving

- Physical access controls eg passwords, keeping doors locked, restricting access to payroll and the bank account so that only staff that need access to particular functions are provided with it

2.2.1 Passwords

All users of a computerised accounting system should have a password that gives them access only to the parts of the system they are authorised to use. This means staff cannot complete operations that are not related to their role.

Passwords should:

- Not be written down
- Not be comprehensible eg 'password' or 'MyName'
- Be kept confidential
- Be changed frequently
- Be strong

A strong password:

- Comprises eight or more characters
- Contains a mix of:
    - Numbers
    - Lower and upper case letters
    - At least one special character such as @ or #

Activity 3: Passwords

The manager of an accounting function is in the process of implementing a new accounting system. All staff are being provided with passwords to access the parts of the system necessary to perform their work.

Think about the possible consequences of poor controls on passwords.

Required:

(a) What rules should be put in place regarding the use and controls of passwords?

(b) Why are these important?

BPP
LEARNING MEDIA

3 Flowcharting an accounting system

All information system processes consist of inputs being processed into outputs. Each stage of the process can be analysed in detail to draw up a simple **system flowchart** that clearly shows the flow of the system using boxes and text.

Illustration 1

In a payroll system:

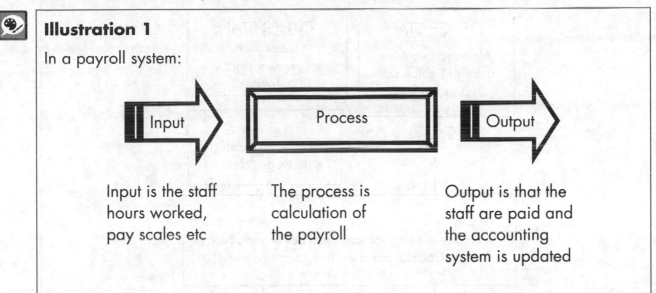

Input	Process	Output
Input is the staff hours worked, pay scales etc	The process is calculation of the payroll	Output is that the staff are paid and the accounting system is updated

Illustration 2

Reading through the CCC scenario at the end of this Course Book, it is straightforward to complete a simple system flowchart of its payroll system as follows:

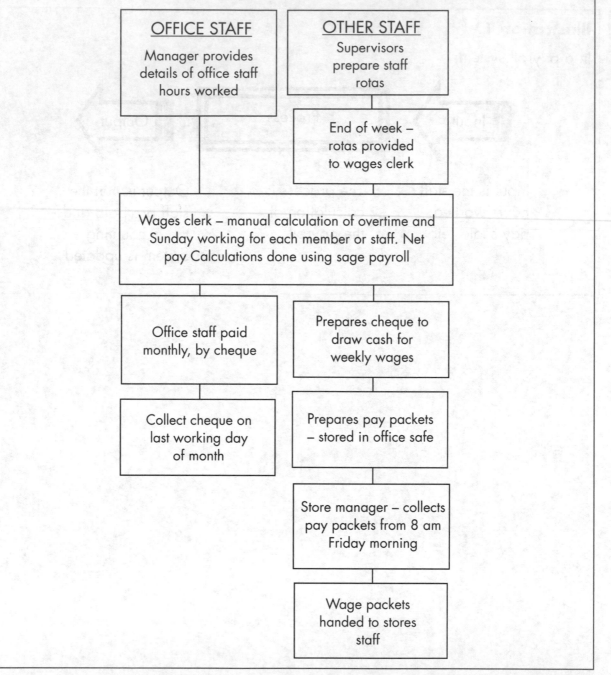

When completing a system flowchart the aim is to map out the system process as accurately as possible. Not all the information required may be available. For example, the flowchart set out above assumes that the manager must provide details of office staff working hours. This is not explicit in the scenario itself.

Completing a system flowchart enables some improvements to the system and to the company to be identified.

BPP
LEARNING MEDIA

Activity 4: Accounts payable system

Have a look at the CCC scenario at the back of this Course Book again.

Required:

(a) Complete a system flowchart for the accounts payable function.

(b) Using your flowchart, identify some recommendations to improve the accounts payable and payroll systems for CCC.

4 SWOT analysis

A key tool for analysing the accounting system in detail is a **SWOT analysis**. SWOT stands for:

- **S**trengths
- **W**eaknesses
- **O**pportunities
- **T**hreats

The strengths and weaknesses of a system will be internal factors.

Illustration 3

A key strength in a payroll system might be that it is operated by knowledgeable and experienced staff. A major weakness might be that it is a manual process, dependent on manual calculation which presents many opportunities for human error.

Once strengths and weaknesses have been identified then recommendations can be made to address the weaknesses.

Opportunities and threats are external to the actual system itself. Taking a payroll system once again:

- There may be an opportunity to train more staff in payroll qualifications.

- A threat would be that information and legislation relating to payroll is always subject to frequent change (tax codes, tax rates, NI contributions etc).

It is sometimes harder to identify external factors such as these, but doing so helps to identify recommendations to improve the system.

Activity 5: SWOT analysis

Have a look at the CCC scenario at the back of this Course Book again.

Required:

Complete a SWOT analysis for CCC using the format below, focusing on the strengths and weaknesses of the internal accounting systems, and the opportunities and threats for the company as a whole.

Strengths

Weaknesses

Opportunities

Threats

BPP
LEARNING MEDIA

5 PEST analysis

A final tool for analysing an accounting system is a PEST analysis. This investigates four factors that may affect the company and its accounting system:

- **P**olitical factors
- **E**conomic factors
- **S**ocial factors
- **T**echnological factors

Political factors – there are a variety of political factors that can affect the operation of an accounting system. These might include:

- Changes in NIC rates
- Changes in VAT rates
- Changes in company legislation regarding the publication of financial statements
- Changes in accounting standards

Economic factors – examples of economic factors that might affect the accounting system are:

- Changes in the volume of transactions due to general or specific changes in the economy and customer demands
- Changes in the availability and wage rate of the labour force
- Whether staff are available to work in the accounting function
- The budget applied to the accounting function

General or specific economic changes may lead to an increase or decrease in the general level of transactions of a company. This will have a direct effect on the number of transactions within an accounting system although not necessarily on the nature of those transactions or the method of operations.

Social factors – social factors that might affect the accounting system could include the following:

- Changing work patterns such as flexitime and home working
- Family commitments leading to changes such as part-time working and job sharing
- Employment legislation

Technological factors – examples of technological factors that might cause changes in the accounts system might be:

- Advances in computer technology
- Security issues
- Technological fraud
- Online banking

6 The culture of the accounting function

The accounting function is not just the accounting system plus the employees who operate it. A key element of any accounting function is the culture that exists within it.

Culture is 'the way we do things around here'. It may be very different from the way a company might ideally want it to be.

Managers and owners set the standard for the accounting function because they operate it on a day-to-day basis, and therefore determine its culture. This is often what makes one company and its accounting function different from another.

The culture of the accounting function may be:

- Based on teamwork – where everyone helps each other to ensure all tasks are completed on time and appropriately by the team as a whole

- Based on individualism – where each member of staff keeps to their own roles and responsibilities

- Based on control – where all rules and procedures are adhered to at all times

- Laissez-faire (relaxed) – where controls are informal and trust is an important part of the controls in place

No one culture is right or wrong, but a particular culture may be inappropriate to the accounting function in question eg a laissez-faire culture in respect of cash is always risky!

Factors affecting the culture of a company and its accounting function include:

- History of the organisation
- Ownership
- Industry the organisation is in
- Management
- Customer expectations
- Size
- Technology
- Rules and procedures
- Structure
- Aims and objectives

BPP LEARNING MEDIA

7 Ethics and the accounting system

Key term

Ethics	A set of generally accepted principles that guide behaviour.
Ethical values	Assumptions and beliefs about what constitutes 'right' and 'wrong' behaviour.

Individuals have **ethical values**, often reflecting the beliefs of the families, cultures and educational environments in which they developed their ideas.

Companies also have ethical values, based on the norms and standards of behaviour that their leaders believe will best help them express their identity and achieve their objectives. Often the values of the company are set out in its mission statement.

Companies are responsible for their actions and are held accountable for the effects of their actions on people and society.

An individual company should behave ethically towards the employees, customers, suppliers and communities affected by them.

7.1 Fundamental principles of professional ethics

The AAT's *Code of Professional Ethics* (the AAT Code) sets out the five **fundamental principles of professional ethics** that underpin the ethical behaviour of a professional accountant in an accounting function:

Fundamental ethical principle	Explanation
Integrity	Accountants must be straightforward and honest in all professional and business relationships.
Objectivity	Accountants must not allow bias, conflict of interest or undue influence of others to override professional or business relationships.
Professional competence and due care	Accountants must maintain professional knowledge and skill at the level required to ensure that a client or employer receives a competent professional service based on current developments in practice, legislation and techniques. They must act diligently and in accordance with applicable and professional standards when providing professional services.

Fundamental ethical principle	Explanation
Confidentiality	Accountants must, in accordance with the law, respect the confidentiality of information acquired as a result of professional and business relationships and not disclose any such information to third parties without proper and specific authority unless there is a legal or professional right or duty to disclose. Confidential information acquired as a result of professional and business relationships shall not be used for the personal advantage of an accountant or third parties.
Professional behaviour	Accountants must comply with relevant laws and regulations and avoid any action that brings the profession into disrepute.

We will look at each of these in turn.

7.2 Integrity

Integrity involves the accountant and the accounting function:

- Being open about the limitations of their knowledge or competence

- Being honest in their relationships

- Carrying out their work accurately, conscientiously and efficiently (cost-effectively)

- Not being associated with false or misleading information

- Not leaving out or obscuring information if it is misleading to do so

One of the key purposes of the accounting function and its accounting system is to provide the necessary information for its internal and external stakeholders. It follows that integrity is probably its most important ethical principle: it should not provide, or even be associated with, misleading information.

7.3 Objectivity

Objectivity means that all professional and business judgements should be made fairly:

- On the basis of an **independent** and intellectually honest appraisal of information

- **Free from** all forms of **prejudice** and **bias**

- Free from factors that might affect **impartiality**, such as pressure from a superior, financial interest in the outcome, a personal or professional relationship with one of the parties involved, or a conflict of interest (where one party stands to lose and another to gain by a particular disclosure)

This principle protects the interests of:

BPP
LEARNING MEDIA

- The parties directly affected by an accountant's services (internal stakeholders plus 'connected' external ones such as banks, suppliers and customers)
- The general public and other external stakeholders who rely on the accuracy of information and the integrity of financial systems

Accountants and the accounting function need to preserve their objectivity by:

- Not letting personal relationships cloud their judgement
- Not accepting, or even considering acceptance of, gifts and hospitality that could be construed as being offered to influence their professional work

7.4 Professional competence and due care

Accountants have to know what they are doing – and to do it right!

Accountants need to:

- Attain then maintain professional knowledge and skill
- Be diligent (act in accordance with the requirements of an assignment, carefully, thoroughly and on a timely basis)
- Apply sound judgement
- Ensure that those working under them have appropriate training and supervision
- Make it clear when they are expressing an opinion and when they are asserting a fact

The accounting function needs to follow the same principle: it should not carry out a task if it cannot do it to a satisfactory standard. To do so may require more resources.

Due care is a legal concept that means that, having agreed to do a task, an accountant must carry it out:

- To the best of their ability
- In the best interests of their client or employer
- Within reasonable timescales
- With proper regard for the technical and professional standards expected

As the experts in the field, accountants may often deal with others, including business owners and other managers, who have little or no knowledge of accounting matters. This puts the accountant in a position of responsibility; they must not carry out the task or assignment in a negligent or 'careless' way.

7.5 Confidentiality

The ethical principle of confidentiality means that the accountant must not:

- Disclose confidential information (ie information acquired as a result of professional and business relationships) unless they have either specific authority to disclose or a legal or professional right or duty to disclose

- Use confidential information to their personal advantage or the advantage of third parties

Staff members in the accounting function should treat as confidential:

- The company's own information

- Personal information shared with the accounting function by employees, customers or suppliers unless told otherwise; this is an important basis for trust in any working relationship

Keeping personal information supplied by third parties confidential is also a legal duty for the company as a data user under the Data Protection Act 1998.

7.6 Professional behaviour

The final ethical principle of professional behaviour means that an accountant must:

- Comply with relevant laws and regulations

- Avoid doing anything that brings disrepute on the accounting profession in the eyes of a reasonable and informed third party

Applying this principle means 'being professional':

- Comply with the law

- Behave in a way that maintains or enhances the reputation of the profession (bringing it credit – not discredit)

- Behave with courtesy and consideration towards everyone

8 Identifying ethical issues

Let us consider some ethical issues concerning Wajid (a part-qualified accounting technician) and his employer's accounting function in line with these fundamental principles.

Illustration 4

Wajid is asked to produce an aged receivables listing for his manager as soon as possible. However, he does not have up-to-date figures because of a problem with the computer system. A colleague suggests that to get the report done in time he should use averages for the missing figures.

There is an **integrity** issue here. Using averages instead of actual figures will almost certainly result in an inaccurate listing.

Wajid should report the problem to his manager and ask for an extension to the deadline in order to provide an accurate listing.

BPP LEARNING MEDIA

Illustration 5

Wajid has opened a letter from an estate agent requesting financial information about one of his company's customers that is applying to rent a property. The information is needed as soon as possible, by email, in order to secure approval for the rent agreement.

There is a **confidentiality** issue here. Wajid needs the customer's authority to disclose the information; he may also need to confirm the identity of the person making the request. He should also take steps to protect the security of the information when he sends it: for example, not using email (which can be intercepted), and stating clearly that the information is confidential.

There is also a **professional behaviour** issue: to comply with the Data Protection Act 1998 it is likely that Wajid's company has rules about what to do on receipt of such a request.

Wajid should not divulge any information without checking with a manager that he is legally allowed to do so.

Illustration 6

A friend tells Wajid on a night out that she expects to inherit money from a recently deceased uncle. She asks him how she will be affected by inheritance tax, capital gains tax and other matters.

There are issues of **professional competence and due care** here. Wajid is not qualified to give advice on matters of taxation. Even if he were qualified, any answer he gives on the spot would risk being incomplete or inaccurate with potentially serious consequences.

Illustration 7

A supplier is so pleased with how promptly Wajid paid him that she offers him a free weekend break in a luxury hotel, just as a 'thank you'.

There is an **objectivity** issue here as the gift is of significant value. Think about how it looks: a third party observer is entitled to wonder what 'special favours' deserve this extra reward – and/or how such a gift may bias Wajid when making payments to the supplier in future.

Activity 6: Ethics and the accounting system

Refer to the CCC scenario at the end of this Course Book.

Required:

(a) Complete a review of ethics within CCC's accounting system, focusing on the five fundamental principles.

(b) Detail any breach, or potential breach, of the five principles that has taken place and explain which principle the actions breach.

(c) Recommend alternative actions that should be taken to prevent the breach occurring.

9 Sustainability

Sustainability is concerned with ensuring a company's activities can continue into the long term without damage to society, the environment or future generations.

Because they must act in the public interest, accountants have a duty to consider the economic, social and environmental aspects of their work in order to support sustainability.

BPP
LEARNING MEDIA

The diagram below shows how economic, social and environmental issues are linked.

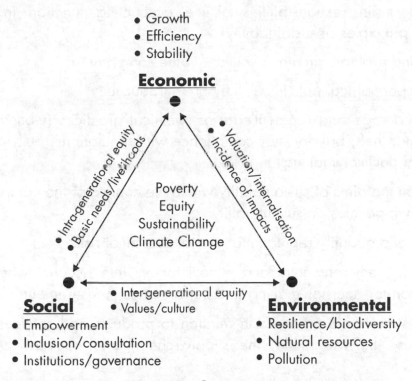

In relation to their work in an accounting function, an accountant must consider:

- Economic aspects:

    - Supporting their company to be profitable

    - Looking for ways to improve the efficiency of the accounting function and the company generally

- Social aspects:

    - Supporting policies on corporate governance

    - Supporting local businesses when deciding on suppliers and paying them on time

    - Consulting the local community when making decisions on investing in or relocating operations

- Environmental aspects:

    - Supporting their company to use less energy, reduce pollution and manage resources and relationships with a view of the long term

    - Running the accounting function in a sustainable manner eg not printing emails unless necessary, turning lights off at the end of the day and recycling materials used in the office

9.1 Responsibilities of the accounting function

There are six main responsibilities of the accounting function in regards to upholding the principles of sustainability:

- Create and promote an ethical culture in the company

    - Support ethical policies as they are introduced

    - Discourage and report illegal or unethical practices (money laundering, fraud, theft, bribery, non-compliance with regulations, bullying and short-term decision-making

- Champion the aims of sustainability within the context of the company's culture and its own policies on sustainability

- Evaluate and quantify reputational and other ethical risks

- Take social, environmental and ethical factors into account when preparing information for decision-making and performance measurement

- Promote sustainable practices in relation to products and services, customers, employees, the workplace, the supply chain, and business functions and processes

- Raise awareness of social responsibility

BPP
LEARNING MEDIA

Chapter summary

- The accounting system processes raw data on transactions into outputs to meet the information needs of stakeholders.

- An effective accounting system: operates effectively; reports accurately; complies with applicable laws and regulations.

- In a centralised accounting system all processes are integrated; in a decentralised system processes operate independently of each other.

- The accounting system includes sub-systems for: payroll; sales ledger; purchases ledger; cash book; general ledger; petty cash; costing.

- Controls in an accounting system allow it to effectively and accurately meet internal and external regulations, and the information needs of stakeholders.

- A user manual documents the accounting system and enables its effectiveness to be kept under review.

- Threats to the accounting system's security include: human error; data loss; malicious damage; fraud.

- Security controls include controls on integrity of data and processing, on the system itself, and on physical access to the system.

- Using and updating strong passwords are key security controls.

- Flowcharting the accounting system and internal controls enables the system's analysis to see whether controls are working effectively.

- SWOT (strengths, weaknesses, opportunities, threats) and PEST (political, economic, social, technological) analysis also help with analysing the accounting system.

- Culture is 'the way we do things round here' and affects how well the accounting system operates.

- The fundamental principles of professional ethics are: integrity; objectivity; professional competence and due care; confidentiality; professional behaviour.

- The accounting system needs to be operated in an ethical manner, following the five fundamental principles, in order to meet its objectives.

- A company is sustainable if it can continue into the long term without damaging society, the environment or future generations.

- The accounting function supports sustainability within the company by: promoting an ethical culture; championing the aims of sustainability within the company; evaluating ethical risks; taking sustainability factors into account when preparing information for decision-making and performance measurement; promoting sustainable practices; raising awareness of social responsibility.

Keywords

- **Accounting system:** A system that takes raw data as its input, processes this, and then produces many outputs.

- **Confidentiality:** Not disclosing confidential information except in appropriate circumstances, and not profiting from confidential information.

- **Culture:** 'The way we do things round here'.

- **Ethical values:** Assumptions and beliefs about what constitutes 'right' and 'wrong' behaviour.

- **Ethics:** A set of generally accepted principles that guide behaviour.

- **Fundamental principles of professional ethics:** The principles that underpin how a professional accountant should behave.

- **Integrated accounting system:** All the data is stored and processed at a central location.

- **Integrity:** Being straightforward and honest in all professional and business relationships.

- **Objectivity:** Not allowing bias, conflict of interest or undue influence of others to override professional or business relationships.

- **PEST analysis:** An analysis of the political, economic, social and technological factors affecting a system.

- **Professional behaviour:** Complying with relevant laws and regulations and not bringing disrepute on the accounting profession.

- **Professional competence and due care:** Having the right level of current professional knowledge and skill to give competent professional service, and acting diligently and in accordance with applicable and professional standards.

- **Security controls:** Controls in the accounting system that cover integrity controls, system controls and physical access controls.

- **Sustainability:** Being able to continue into the long term without damage to society, the environment or future generations.

- **SWOT analysis:** An analysis of a system's strengths, weaknesses, opportunities and threats.

- **System:** Any function that takes an input, processes it, and then produces an output.

- **System flowchart:** A diagram that shows the flow of the accounting system using boxes and text.

- **Systemic weaknesses:** Weaknesses that arise within the accounting system itself, which leave it open to fraud and error.

- **User manual:** An accurate analysis of how the accounting system and its controls operate, and how they should be used.

BPP LEARNING MEDIA

Activity answers

Activity 1: Centralisation of the accounting system

(a) Advantages for CCC of a centralised system might include:

- All data is stored in one central place so greater control
- Improved security
- Staff can all use the same system leading to efficiencies in training etc
- Centralised reporting
- Consistent reporting
- Quicker access to information

(b) Advantages of a decentralised system might include:

- Each individual system can be more relevant to that area of the company's needs

- Lower risk of errors/breakdowns affecting the whole company

- Lower-level staff might have more control and autonomy over their system thus improving morale

- Quicker access to information from each individual system

(c) CCC is better suited to a centralised system so that all staff can be trained to use one system and can then cover each other's roles or access information if required. It will also enable financial reports to be quickly and easily provided to the owner for management decision-making.

Activity 2: Documentation of controls

(a) Advantages of a user manual for Hinton Ltd's accounting system:

- Quick and efficient training of new staff
- Better visibility of the controls in place
- Consistent approach to completing activities
- Easier to rotate staff between roles and responsibilities
- Easier to evaluate staff
- Improved supervisory and management control
- More effective time management

(b) Disadvantages of a user manual:

- Increased risk of 'outsiders' being able to operate the system

- Procedures may stifle innovation and improvements to processes

- User manuals take time to complete

- The manuals may become out of date quickly

BPP
LEARNING MEDIA

- The manuals need to be tested to ensure they accurately reflect the systems in place

- Staff often do not conform to manuals, negating the benefits of having them

Activity 3: Passwords

(a) The company might put in place the following rules regarding the use and control of passwords.

- Passwords must not be written down

- Passwords must not be shared

- Passwords must be changed regularly

- Passwords must not be generic

- When staff leave, access must be cancelled on the day they leave the department

- Access can only be set up for new staff with management authorisation

- Staff access to different parts of the system must be regularly reviewed

(b) These rules and controls protect the integrity of the system and the company. If one password is used by all staff (generic) then there is little point in using them as the whole system is open to all. This lack of control then increases the risk of errors, from staff using parts of the system they are not trained to use, and fraud.

Access to the system should be controlled so that staff are not granted access to parts they do not require. If staff leave their access should be cancelled immediately so they cannot continue to use the system, and other staff cannot use their passwords. Often companies make sharing of passwords a disciplinary offence to ensure that controls are maintained.

BPP
LEARNING MEDIA

Activity 4: Accounts payable system

(a) System flowchart for the accounts payable function:

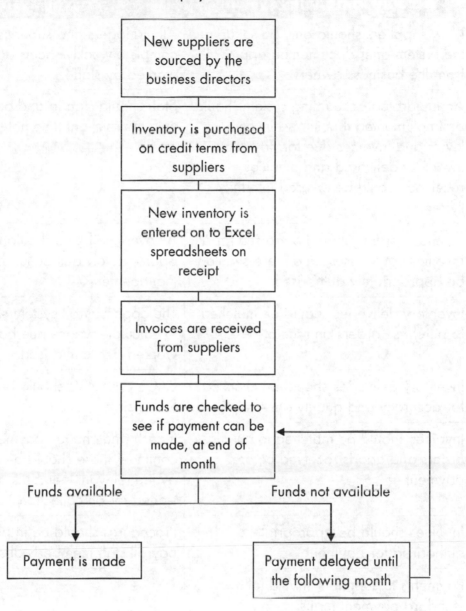

(b) Recommendations to improve the accounts payable and payroll systems might include:

Accounts payables system	Payroll system
New suppliers should only be set up on the system after documented approval from the business owners	All managers and supervisors should complete weekly sheets on actual hours worked by staff
An integrated accounting system should be implemented that shows inventory levels and invoices due for payment. Inventory delivered and invoices received should be entered into this system	Staff should sign in and out of work, with the relevant time noted
Purchase orders should be raised for all inventory purchases, and these should be appropriately authorised	All overtime hours should be appropriately authorised by management
Inventory deliveries should be matched to purchase orders on receipt	The Sage payroll system should be used to calculate wages due based on hours worked and authorised
Inventory deliveries should be checked for accuracy and quality on receipt	BACS payments should be implemented for all staff
Invoices should be matched to purchase orders and goods received before payment	If cash and cheque payments are to continue, these should be collected only by the relevant members of staff and signed for on collection
Invoices should be appropriately authorised for payment	Procedures should be in place to cover payroll staff member's absence
Payments to suppliers should follow standard payment terms	

BPP
LEARNING MEDIA

Activity 5: SWOT analysis

Sometimes answers can be down to interpretation, especially between strengths and opportunities, and weaknesses and threats. Do not worry about which heading you listed each under, it is enough that you identified them.

An example SWOT analysis for CCC might include the following:

Strengths	Weaknesses
• An open plan accounts office ensures that when staff are in and working with each other they can communicate freely and cover each other's work when absent. • The cheque book is kept in a locked desk in the office – but see weaknesses. • Current inventory system has good detail included. • Credit reference agency used to decide whether to grant credit. • Some credit control procedures are in place. • Controls re cash and cheques coming into the office – manual day book then accounts. • Staff seem keen to improve systems – Accounts Receivable Clerk has implemented some initiatives. • Cash movement is reduced by using cash to make up wages.	• As most accounts staff are part-time there are often occasions when no one is in the office. The door is generally propped open; there is a risk members of the public could access the office. • As all staff can access the office and the accounting system with common passwords, there is a lack of control. There will also be issues concerning communication between staff as they are not all in the office at the same time. • Stand-alone computers, with no central system or database, reduces the ability to produce meaningful reports for key stakeholders. • Staff, as a whole, are not qualified in accounting, which poses a risk of errors and relaxed controls and also a lack of accountability. • There appears to be a lack of planning in the work of the accounting team, highlighted by the fact that when the payroll was first brought in-house a temping agency was contracted to run it for the first two months. This could have led to errors and inconsistencies in the work and the handover of the system to the Wages Clerk once employed. • Stores staff are paid in cash which poses a risk of theft. • Office staff are paid by cheque – the frequent use of cheques can lead to the risk of cheques being stolen and fraudulently used.

Strengths	Weaknesses
	• Manual calculation of weekly payroll with no secondary check is a weakness as it can lead to errors or fraudulent increases in staff pay.
	• Wages are paid in cash – any use of cash poses a risk of theft.
	• Overdue debts are often not followed up beyond an initial phone call.
	• The cheque book is kept in an easily accessible drawer that is sometimes left unlocked.
	• Staff are not trained in Excel, increasing the risk of errors.
	• New credit customers are not given a realistic credit limit.
	• Invoices are produced using Word – this has potential for errors.
	• Cash is not counted when removed from the tills on weekdays.
	• No controls over petty cash and over cash taken from tills.
	• No contingency planning – accounting staff are not able to take on each other's roles when absent.
	• Staff are unable to cover each other's roles as they lack the skills to do so.
	• No control on authorisation – signing of blank cheques to cover absence.
	• No controls on payments to suppliers or payments from customers.
	• Payments to suppliers are made without checking systems or informing other staff.
	• Lack of controls on staff hours have led to incorrect rotas and staff pay.
	• Pay packets for more than one pay period can be completed in one go – this is a weakness as too much cash was in the office.
	• Wages should be completed correctly each week, not in advance and adjusted later.

BPP
LEARNING MEDIA

Opportunities	Threats
• There is an opportunity to use one central accounting system on networked computers, which will ensure there is better cover for work when staff are absent and better reporting of key financial information to relevant stakeholders.	• Using spreadsheet software (Excel) to prepare accounts poses a risk of errors being made in formulas that are difficult to spot, resulting in incorrect inventory and accounting information.
• There is an opportunity to train staff in accounting and also in the systems they use, making them much more aware of the controls and procedures they should be operating and also more efficient.	• The use of one common password is a threat to systems and the data held within them (for example through unauthorised access).
• There is an opportunity to train staff in each other's roles – perhaps with a backup member of staff for each. This could motivate staff and also ensure cover during absence.	• The lack of formal procedures and controls has contributed to extensive use of the overdraft facility and caused the bank concern. This is a cash flow threat to the company.
• There is an opportunity to outsource the payroll function to the company accountants.	• There appears to be no backup taken of the current systems. This is a threat because key financial data would be lost if the systems failed.
	• Regulatory environment – this is constantly changing, for example potential changes to VAT rates. The accounting system needs to be able to recognise these changes and react accordingly.
	• Debt collection – while a relationship with a debt collection agency is in place, this is rarely used due to the costs involved. This may mean that debts are never recovered.

Activity 6: Ethics and the accounting system

(a) Current practice	(b) Principle breached and details	(c) Recommended practice
Disclosure of personal details (address and telephone number) of a member of staff to an individual on the telephone.	CONFIDENTIALITY The law requires accountants to respect the confidentiality of information acquired as a result of professional and business relationships and not disclose such information to third parties without proper and specific authority unless there is a legal or professional right or duty to disclose.	Personal details of staff should be stored in accordance with the Data Protection Act and not disclosed without the permission of the employee in question, unless there is a legal or professional right or duty to disclose.
Christmas party bill was split in order to get around HMRC tax deductible expense limits.	PROFESSIONAL BEHAVIOUR By asking the Accounts Payable Clerk to breach HMRC rules in relation to the bill for the Christmas party, the director failed to comply with relevant laws and regulations. By failing to confront the director rather than carry out the request, the Accounts Payable Clerk assisted the director in breaching this principle.	• The full £160 per head does not qualify as a tax deductible expense and as such should not be treated as one. • HMRC rules should be fully complied with at all times.

BPP LEARNING MEDIA

(a) Current practice	(b) Principle breached and details	(c) Recommended practice
A director asked a member of staff to produce a set of financial statements that show the company in the 'best possible light' in order to secure a bank loan.	INTEGRITY Producing financial statements designed to mislead the bank as to the position of the company represents a lack of honesty. To comply with the fundamental principle of integrity, a member must be straightforward and honest in all professional and business relationships.	• Accounts should be prepared that show a true and fair view of the company's financial performance and position.
A director placed an exceptionally large order with a supplier on the basis that the supplier had promised to sponsor a motorcycle show if the order was increased. The director has a favourite group of suppliers, mainly because they are sometimes willing to sponsor his motorbike and racing efforts.	OBJECTIVITY Bias, conflict of interest or undue influence of others should not override professional or business relationships. The director is allowing conflict of interest to affect his professional relationships and judgement. Suppliers should be selected based on the value for money they can offer, not on personal favours offered in exchange for the business.	• A formal approved supplier list should be established. • Where an approved supplier is not in place, a minimum of three quotes should be obtained and the supplier that offers the best value for money should be chosen.

1 **Complete the following statement.**

An integrated accounting system is **(1)** _____. One of its core objectives should be **(2)** _____.

Picklists:

(1) centralised/decentralised
(2) compliance with laws and regulations/cost control

2 **Identify whether each of the following control activities is an integrity, system or physical access security control.**

Activities	Type of security control
Validation of input data	Physical access control
Passwords	System control
Archiving	Integrity control

3 **Which of the following is the most secure password for use in an accounting system?**

password	
TekfU4af#	
2468TTfn	
The/password@	

4 **Complete the following statement.**

In SWOT analysis, strengths and weaknesses are _____ and opportunities and threats are _____.

Picklist:

external to the company
internal to the company

5 **Complete the following statement.**

The requirement for an accountant to act diligently is part of the fundamental principle of

integrity.	
professional competence and due care.	
professional behaviour.	
objectivity.	

BPP
LEARNING MEDIA

Internal control
systems

4

Learning outcomes

2.1	**Discuss how internal controls can support the organisation**
	• Explain the purpose of internal controls
	• Assess how a strong system of internal controls can minimise the risk of loss to an organisation
	• Assess how a strong system of internal controls can ensure ethical standards in an organisation
	• Identify the types of internal controls used in different parts of the accounting function
	• Consider how different types of internal controls suit different types of organisations
2.3	**Examine ways of preventing and detecting fraud and systemic weaknesses**
	• The common types of systemic weaknesses and their causes
	• The need for segregation of duties
	• The role of internal controls in preventing fraud and errors
	• The role of internal controls in detecting fraud and errors
3.2	**Evaluate the underpinning procedures of an accounting system, assessing the impact on the operation of the organisation**
	• Identify how underpinning procedures in the organisation impact on the operation of the organisation (payroll, authorisation and control of sales, purchases, capital expenditure, overheads, payments and receipts)
	• Identify how underpinning procedures in the organisation can support ethical standards and sustainability practices
	• Identify weaknesses in the underpinning procedures and the impact on cost-effectiveness, reliability and timeliness
	• Evaluate the impact of weaknesses in the underpinning procedures in terms of time, money and reputation

Assessment context

Assessment of these topics will be included within a number of tasks in the synoptic assessment at Level 4.

Qualification context

How the bookkeeping controls discussed in this chapter operate is covered at both Level 2 and Level 3.

Business context

The internal control system is designed to ensure the company does not fall prey to fraud, error or misstatement of its financial statements. This ensures that the company can operate effectively.

BPP LEARNING MEDIA

Chapter overview

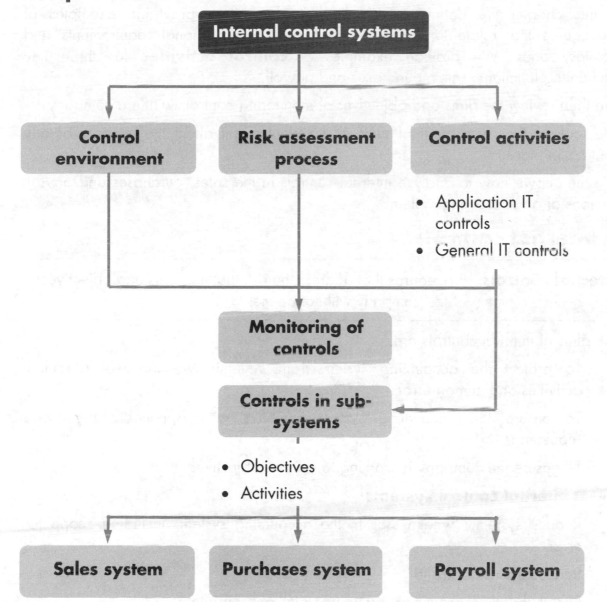

Introduction

In this chapter we define **internal controls** further, providing examples of procedures that relate to the meeting of both organisational requirements and statutory ones. We provide examples of **control activities** for three key accounting functions: sales, purchases and payroll.

We then review the aims and objectives of monitoring controls within a company.

We look at the assessment of **risk** and how it might affect the integrity of any controls in place.

We then cover how to analyse internal controls in the sales, purchases and payroll sections of an accounting system.

1 Internal controls

> **Internal controls** Procedures that address the risk that the aims and objectives of the company will not be met.

Key term

The aims of internal controls are:

- To protect the accounting system from systemic weaknesses, fraudulent activities and human error
- To ensure the accounting system complies with applicable laws and regulations
- To ensure the company is working to meet its objectives

Robust **internal control systems**:

- Reduce systemic weaknesses in the accounting system, including scope for error
- Reduce the risk of fraud
- Ensure that the accounting system operates appropriately
- Ensures the accounting system can change in line with the environment and organisational requirements

An internal control system consists of:

- The **control environment**
- The **risk assessment process**
- Control activities
- Monitoring of controls

BPP
LEARNING MEDIA

2 The control environment

Key term

Control environment	Formed by the attitudes, awareness and actions of management and those responsible for ensuring that the internal controls within the company meet that company's needs.

The control environment Is the foundation on which the internal control system rests.

The owners or management of a company can introduce numerous controls to ensure that nothing goes wrong, but if everyone ignores them, and management do nothing about that, then the internal control system will not operate.

Indications of a good control environment:

- Management communicate and enforce integrity and ethical behaviour

- Management and staff are well trained and competent

- Management operates in a way that promotes control

- The company and accounting function is structured in a way that promotes control

- Authority and responsibility for controls is assigned to people

- Human resources policies promote controls

The size of a company will have an impact on the control environment.

Activity 1: The control environment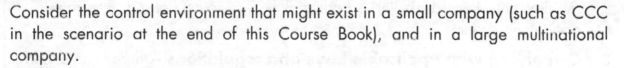

Consider the control environment that might exist in a small company (such as CCC in the scenario at the end of this Course Book), and in a large multinational company.

Required:

Identify ways in which the control environment will be affected by the size of the company.

3 The risk assessment process

The internal control system must respond to risks that:

- Objectives might not be met, including the company's sustainability and CSR objectives

- The company may be the victim of fraud

- The system may contain errors that result in misstatement in the financial statements

- The company is engaged in unethical behaviour

- The company fails to comply with its legal obligations

A robust risk assessment process needs to be in place to reduce or avoid risks.

Illustration 1

A risk assessment of CCC's accounting system in the scenario at the end of this Course Book shows it has the following risks with regard to its objectives:

1 **Operating effectively** – members of the accounting team are not all in the office at the same time; most are part-time and work different days. The directors have recently been absent from work without adequate cover. If one of the directors or members of the accounting team were to become ill there is no adequate cover. The company operates with few formal controls and is based on trust in the integrity of staff.

2 **Reporting accurately** – the owners and most of the accounting team have no formal accounting qualifications and therefore no knowledge of reporting requirements. Record-keeping is poor and there is no centralised, integrated accounting system.

3 **Complying with applicable laws and regulations** – there is no expert in accounting and payroll regulations and no person responsible for ensuring the business remains up to date with regulations and laws.

The risk assessment process throws up details of how risks are being mitigated (or not!).

BPP LEARNING MEDIA

Illustration 2

Taking CCC's accounting system again:

1   **Operating effectively** – the directors left signed cheques to be used during their absence, so that suppliers and staff could continue to be paid, and have now employed one full-time member of staff in the accounting function.

2   **Reporting accurately** – that there are no formal accounting qualifications held by the staff was partly mitigated by the use of a third party to complete the payroll (a highly regulated function), but this is no longer the case. The directors are keen to support staff who wish to train and obtain qualifications, but leave them to organise this themselves.

3   **Complying with applicable laws and regulations** – very little has been done here according to the scenario. It does mention that the company has a firm of accountants, Southampton Accounting Services, and it could be that they provide appropriate advice regarding accounting regulations and payroll law.

3.1 Size and type of company

Clearly the risks facing a particular company and its accounting system will be unique. They will be affected by:

- The size of the company
- Whether it operates in a highly regulated industry or not

A small company may rely on advice from external sources (eg a payroll bureau) while a larger one will rely more on internal staff to assess risk.

Activity 2: Risk assessment process

Metal Extrusions Midlands Ltd (MEM) is a family business which is 80 years old. It has six family members on the board of directors, four of whom are active in the business. It employs 50 staff: 40 in manufacturing, 10 in administration. The administration department includes an accounting function with a staff of five, including a Financial Controller. The Financial Controller is a qualified accountant and is not on the board of directors. None of the directors has any accounting skills.

MEM produces metal extrusions, which is a highly mechanised operation. It has always carried out its operations in the same factory. The factory and its machinery are very old. MEM made a significant investment in new machinery in 1954. There have been few developments in metal extrusion since that time. However, the company has been experiencing competition in recent years from a new company set up by two disgruntled former employees.

MEM has several suppliers of metals and the other materials required for production. There are two major suppliers, one of which is British and the other

French. The company purchases 30% of its metal raw materials from the French supplier, which insists on invoicing and being paid in euros.

Required:

Identify as many risks as you can, particularly with regard to the objectives of (a) operating effectively, (b) reporting accurately and (c) complying with applicable laws and regulations.

4 Control activities

Control activities The policies and procedures that help ensure that objectives are carried out.

Key term

Types of control activity that should be used in an accounting system to address systemic weaknesses (remember these as SPAMSOAP):

- **S**egregation of duties – making sure that a number of people are involved in different parts of each process to minimise the opportunity for fraud and error eg different members of staff should (1) open the post, (2) record cheques received and (3) bank cheques received.

- **P**hysical controls – controls over the physical security of accounting records and assets such as cash and inventory

- **A**uthorisation (approval) of transactions by supervisors and managers – this shows the person processing the transaction that it is valid

- **M**anagement controls – managers should review: whether activity controls are being carried out within the accounting system; overall performance eg comparing budget to actual performance in a budgetary control report, and comparing performance and position from one period to the next using ratio analysis

- **S**upervisory controls – there should be close oversight of people performing accounting tasks day to day

BPP
LEARNING MEDIA

- **O**rganisation – the way tasks and the business as a whole are organised should support internal control eg clear lines of responsibility, delegation and reporting, and adequate resources being available for the accounting system

- **A**rithmetic and bookkeeping checks on whether transactions have been processed accurately and completely eg **reconciliations**

- **P**ersonnel controls – appropriate accounting staff should be recruited, selected and trained

---

Illustration 3

If an accounts payable clerk is able to raise a purchase order, book goods into inventory, process the supplier's invoice then pay it, they may be able to purchase goods for their own use and pay for them through the company's system. By not allowing the same member of staff access to all of these activities the risk of fraud is significantly reduced.

There are some common specific control activities that are used in many accounting systems (we shall look at these in more detail when we look at sales, purchases and wages):

- **Authorisation** and control of documents: transactions should be approved by an appropriate person; eg overtime should be approved by departmental heads.

- **IT controls**: general controls, or **application controls** built into the IT system.

- **Arithmetical accuracy controls**: eg when invoices are raised or received, a staff member should ensure that the invoice adds up correctly.

- **Accounting controls** eg control accounts and trial balances help to identify mistakes in the accounting records. Remember only some errors result in a trial balance not balancing (unequal amounts double entry error; two debits/two credits entry error; one-sided entry error; balance calculation error; balance transfer error; balance omission).

- **Reconciliations**: reconciling two different sources of information, such as a bank statement and a cash book, or a purchases ledger account and a statement from the supplier, can also highlight if errors have occurred.

- **Comparing assets to records**: eg compare non-current assets held with those recorded as owned in the non-current asset register; compare cash in the petty cash tin with the amount shown in the petty cash book.

- **Restricting access to assets and accounting records**: eg lock receipts in a safe until they go to the bank; have codes to unlock the cash tills; lock the stores where inventory is kept.

In smaller companies, management may be more involved in actually implementing control activities: there may not be enough staff to ensure segregation of controls.

Activity 3: Segregation of duties

Look at the descriptions of the accounting systems at CCC in the scenario at the end of this Course Book. Think about what is appropriate to a company such as CCC, which is small and has limited accounting staff.

Required:

(a) **What do you think of the degree of segregation of duties operating in these systems?**

(b) **Could further segregation be implemented? Think this through carefully and then review the suggested answers at the back of this Workbook.**

4.1 Application IT controls

Key term

Application controls	Controls relating to the transactions and standing data in the computerised accounting system.

IT controls are categorised as:

- Input controls on completeness of data input to the system:

    - Check processed output to source documents on a one-to-one basis

    - Check the number of transactions processed with the number of original documents

    - Check batch totals of the value of the amounts processed between the source documents and the total input to the computer

- Programmed controls on accuracy of data input to the system:

    - Check the plausibility of data input into certain fields eg some fields might be wrong if they were a negative number, or the VAT field might have to be a sensible percentage (20% or 5%) of the total field

    - Check validity of data input eg invoice numbers might have a letter as well as number values to be valid

BPP LEARNING MEDIA

- Authorisation checks to see that the source documentation input has been authorised by suitable personnel

- **Processing controls** eg to warn the user if they try to log out before processing is finished

- Controls over standing data:

  - Regular **reviews** of data to ensure that it is correct eg prices, names, part numbers

  - Programmed controls eg a hash total of the number of personnel on the payroll to ensure no unauthorised amendments have been made

4.2 General IT controls

General IT controls are controls (other than application controls) relating to the computer environment.

They aim to establish a framework of overall control over the system's activities.

General IT controls apply on:

- Developing computer applications

- Preventing unauthorised changes to applications

- Testing genuine changes when they are made

- Segregating duties (other users of the same programmes will notice unauthorised changes)

- Preventing applications being used by the wrong people at the wrong time

- Security – limiting access to computers and software programmes:

  - Physically (by locking them up)
  - By using passwords
  - By creating back-ups of important files and then keeping them safe when they are being developed and tested

We looked at security controls in Chapter 3 as well.

5 Monitoring of controls

Monitoring of controls is necessary to assess the quality of internal control performance over time.

An internal audit function may carry out these controls, but even in smaller companies without a separate internal audit function, effective monitoring can take place, formally or informally, by function heads – eg the sales director is likely to become aware of deficiencies in controls in the sales cycle because it means the sales department does not function as well.

5.1 Limitations of internal control systems

Inherent limitations of effectiveness of controls:

- People make mistakes
- People may not operate controls properly in error
- People may deliberately circumvent control systems if they want to defraud the company

6 Sales system controls

Not all parts of the accounting system have the same internal controls. We are going to look at the types of controls that are found in sales systems and the risks that they are designed to address.

When a company makes cash sales, no credit is granted, so there is no formal order as the customer chooses and pays for goods which are available. Risks associated with cash sales arise in respect of the cash element, which is discussed later.

Here we are focusing mainly on the **control objectives** of the credit sales sub-system, and the risk that is controlled when each control objective is achieved:

- **Control objective**: the correct action that needs to take place eg invoice customers for goods received
- **Risk**: the threat to the company presented by the control objective not be attained eg company loses inventory and does not receive payment for the sale if customers are not invoiced for goods received

6.1 Control objectives in the sales system

Taking orders and extending credit

Control objective	Risk controlled
Only supply goods to customers who are likely to pay for them (customers with a good credit rating)	Company loses goods of value and does not receive value in return
Customers pay promptly	Company cannot use the money in its business Company cannot earn interest on money due to late payment
Record orders correctly	Company sends the wrong goods to the customer, causing added cost or risk of loss of the customer
Fulfil orders promptly	Company loses custom

BPP LEARNING MEDIA

Despatching and invoicing

Control objective	Risk controlled
Record goods sent out	Goods sent out and not invoiced, so the company loses money
Correctly invoice goods and services sold	Insufficient charged and the company loses money
Only invoice goods that have been sent out	Company charges for goods in error and loses custom
Only issue credit notes for a valid reason	Company issues credit notes incorrectly and loses money

Recording and accounting for sales, credit control

Control objective	Risk controlled
Record invoiced sales in the accounting records (sales ledger and general ledger)	Sales not recorded and wrongly omitted from financial statements Payment not chased as the sale was never recorded
Record credit notes in the accounting records	Financial statements misstated Lose custom by chasing cancelled debts
Record invoiced sales in the correct sales ledger accounts	Lose custom by chasing the wrong customer for the debt Not receiving the money from the correct customer
Record invoices in the correct time period	Errors in financial statements due to counting both the debt and the related inventory as assets, or counting neither Penalty from HMRC for recording VAT in the wrong VAT period
Identify debts for which payment might be doubtful	Failure to take action until it is too late to recover the debt Irrecoverable debts misstated as assets in the financial statements

Receiving payment (cash and cheques)

Control objective	Risk controlled
Record all money received	Money could be stolen or lost
	Custom lost through chasing payments already made by the customer
	Financial statements misstated
Bank all money received	Money could be stolen or lost
	Custom lost through chasing payments already made by the customer
	Financial statements misstated
	Company cannot earn interest on money
Safeguard money received until it is banked	Money may be stolen in the interim period

6.2 Controls in the sales system

6.2.1 Segregation of duties

Dividing tasks among several staff members in the sales system, especially in relation to handling cheques and cash receipts, is a key control.

- A person could create a false customer to steal the company's inventory and then not pay for it. This would only be possible if the same person were in charge of orders and credit control/accounts receivable (sales ledgers).

- A person could intercept cheques when they arrive and steal them before they are recorded.

- A person could steal cheques and/or cash and misallocate them to the accounts receivable (sales ledger) records, making it look as if the customer is further behind in payment than is actually the case on an ongoing basis). Such a fraud may not be discovered as the customer may never appear behind enough in payments to be chased for overdue debts.

BPP LEARNING MEDIA

6.2.2 Control activities

The following are some control activities for specific control objectives.

Taking orders and extending credit

Control objective	Control activity
Only supply goods to customers who are likely to pay for them (customers with a good credit rating)	Credit terms should be authorised by senior personnel and reviewed regularly Credit checks should be carried out on new customers Changes in customer data (for example, their address) should be authorised by senior personnel Orders should only be accepted from customers with no existing payment problems
Record orders correctly	Order documents should be sequentially numbered so that 'false sales' can be traced

Despatching and invoicing goods

Control objective	Control activity
Record goods sent out	Despatch of goods should be authorised by appropriate personnel and checked to order documents Despatched goods should be checked for quality and quantity Despatch notes should be agreed to customer orders Despatch notes should be sequentially numbered and the sequence should be checked regularly Inventory records should be updated from goods sent out records Orders not yet processed should be regularly reviewed
Correctly invoice goods and services sold	Invoices should be prepared using authorised prices Invoices should be checked to ensure they add up correctly Invoices should be pre-numbered and the sequence should be checked regularly

Control objective	Control activity
Only invoice goods that have been sent out	Customers should sign despatch notes as proof of receipt Quantities should be checked to despatch notes Sales invoices should be matched with signed delivery notes and sales orders
Only issue credit notes for a valid reason	Returned goods should be checked for quality Returned goods should be recorded on goods returned notes Credit notes should be authorised by appropriate personnel

Recording and accounting for sales, credit control

Control objective	Control activity
Record invoiced sales in the accounting records (sales ledger and general ledger)	Sales invoice sequence should be recorded and spoilt invoices recorded and destroyed
Record credit notes in the accounting records	Sales returns and price adjustments should be recorded separately from the original sale
Record invoiced sales in the correct sales ledger accounts	Receivables statements should be prepared and checked regularly Receivables statements should be safeguarded so they cannot be amended before they are sent out Accounts receivable control account should be reconciled regularly to the sales ledger
Record invoices in the correct time period	Implement cut-off procedure
Identify debts for which payment might be doubtful	Overdue accounts should be reviewed and followed up Write-off of irrecoverable debts should be authorised by appropriate personnel

- Sales receipts should be matched with invoices
- Customer remittance advices should be retained

BPP LEARNING MEDIA

Receiving payment (cash and cheques)

Control objective	Control activity
Record all money received	Protect post received to avoid interception
	Two people should be present at post opening, a list of receipts should be made and post should be stamped with the date opened
	There should be appropriate arrangements made when cashiers are on holiday
	Receipts books should be serially numbered and kept locked up
Bank all money received	Till rolls should be reconciled to cash collections which should then be agreed to cash banked. Cash and cheques should be banked daily
	Paying in books should be compared to initial cash records
	All receipts should be banked together
Safeguard money received until it is banked	There should be restrictions on who is allowed to accept cash (cashiers or sales people)
	Cash received should be evidenced (till rolls, receipts)
	Cash registers should be regularly emptied
	Cash shortages should be investigated. Opening of new bank accounts should be restricted to certain personnel and authorised by senior management
	Cash floats held should be limited
	Restrictions should be in place when making payments from cash received
	Restricted should be in place for access to cash on the premises
	Cash floats should be checked by an independent person, sometimes on a surprise basis
	Cash should be locked up outside normal business hours

Activity 4: Sales system controls (1)

Hinton Ltd has the following controls in its sales system:

(a) Credit checks should be run on new customers.
(b) Sales invoices should be sequentially numbered.
(c) Receivables statements should be prepared regularly.
(d) Restrictions on who is allowed to receive cash.

Required:

What are the objectives of each of the controls?

Activity 5: Sales system controls (2)

At XYZ Ltd, a medium-sized company:

Peter receives sales orders in a variety of ways: by telephone, by email and in person. Whenever he receives an order, he notes it in the sales order book. Some orders can be fulfilled from shop inventory, others must be ordered from suppliers.

When an order is delivered, Peter raises a despatch note on his computer. The computer automatically raises an invoice when a despatch note is raised. These documents are printed off and sent to the customer. When the documents are printed, the software automatically updates the sales day book which is also on the computer.

When customers pay, Peter enters the details of the cheques into the cash book.

Some of the controls in the system have been highlighted. Some of these are manual controls and others are computerised. For instance, orders are manually recorded in the order book, but sales invoices are automatically listed in the sales day book as a result of a computer program.

BPP
LEARNING MEDIA

Required:

List out as many other controls that should exist in XYZ Ltd's system as outlined above as you can.

7 Purchase system controls

The purchases system – from placing an order to paying the supplier's invoice – is a part of the accounting system which it is particularly important to have controls over:

- The purchases system involves receiving inventory and paying cash – arguably the two types of asset which are most open to fraud and theft

- Purchases may be of very high value when the company is incurring capital expenditure in particular

- Information from the purchases system becomes part of the data which supports the costing system. Errors and fraud in purchasing will lead to inaccurate information being used for planning, decision making and performance measurement

7.1 Control objectives in the purchases system

Ordering

Control objective	Risk controlled
Only order goods and services that are authorised by appropriate personnel and are for the company's benefit	Company pays for unnecessary or personal goods
Only order from authorised suppliers	Unauthorised suppliers may not supply quality goods or may be too expensive

Receipt of goods and services

Control objective	Risk controlled
Goods and services received are used for the company purposes	Company may pay for goods/services for personal use
Only accept goods and services that have been ordered (and appropriately authorised)	Company may pay for goods/services for personal use
Record all goods and services received	Company fails to pay for goods/services and loses suppliers
Claim all credits due	Company pays for goods it does not use
Do not accept unwanted goods/services	Company pays for goods it does not use

Accounting

Control objective	Risk controlled
Only make authorised payments for goods that have been received	Company pays for goods it does not use
Record expenses correctly in the accounting records	Financial statements are misstated and the company does not pay for genuine liabilities
Record credit notes received correctly in the accounting records	Financial statements are misstated and the company pays for items unnecessarily
Record liabilities in the correct purchases ledger accounts	Company pays the wrong supplier
Record expenses in the correct period	Financial statements are misstated by recording a purchase but not inventory, or recording inventory but not the associated liability Penalty from HMRC for recording VAT in the wrong VAT period

Payments

Control objective	Risk controlled
Only make payments to the correct recipients and for the correct amounts which are authorised	Company pays the wrong supplier
Only pay for liabilities once	Company pays more than once and the supplier does not correct the mistake

BPP
LEARNING MEDIA

7.2 Controls in the purchases system

7.2.1 Segregation of duties

Once again segregation of duties in a purchases system is vital.

The concern is that a person could order and pay for personal goods through the company, so ordering and payment should be separated.

The risk of fraud will also be reduced if the person who writes out the cheques is different from the person who signs the cheques.

7.2.2 Control activities

The following are some control activities for specific control objectives.

Ordering

Control objective	Control activity
Only order goods and services that are authorised by appropriate personnel and are for the company's benefit	Necessity for orders should be evidenced before orders are authorised
	Only prepare orders when purchase requisitions are received from departments
	Pre-number and safeguard blank order forms. Orders not yet received should be reviewed
Only order from authorised suppliers	Have a central policy for choosing suppliers. Monitor supplier terms and take advantage of discounts offered

Receipt of goods and services

Control objective	Control activity
Goods and services received are used for the company's purposes	Examine for quality and quantity
Only accept goods and services that have been ordered (and appropriately authorised)	Evidence receipt on pre-numbered goods received notes
Record all goods and services received	Check invoices to orders and goods received notes
	Reference invoices (stamp with sequential number and supplier reference)
Claim all credits due	Check invoices for prices, quantities and calculations
	Record goods returned on pre-numbered goods returned notes

Control objective	Control activity
Do not accept unwanted goods/services	Compare goods received notes with purchase orders

Accounting

Control objective	Control activity
Only make authorised payments for goods that have been received	Payments should be authorised
Record expenses correctly in the accounting records	Record promptly in day books and ledgers
Record credit notes received correctly in the accounting records	Record promptly in day books and ledgers
Record liabilities in the correct purchases ledger accounts	Regularly update purchases ledger Compare supplier statements with accounts payable Reconcile control account with list of balances
Record expenses in the correct period	Goods received but not yet invoiced at the year end should be accrued separately

Payments

Control objective	Control activity
Only make payments to the correct recipients and for the correct amounts which are authorised	Cheques should be requisitioned and requests evidenced with supporting documentation Cheque payments should be authorised by someone other than a signatory Limits on the payment amount individual staff members can sign for Blank cheques should never be signed Signed cheques should be despatched promptly Cash payments should be limited and authorised
Only pay for liabilities once	Payments should be recorded promptly in the cash book and ledger

BPP LEARNING MEDIA

Activity 6: Purchases system controls

Hinton Ltd has the following controls in its purchases system:

(a) The necessity for orders should be evidenced.
(b) Supplier invoices should be matched to goods received.
(c) Supplier statements should be compared with accounts payable.
(d) Blank cheques should never be signed.

Required:

What are the objectives of each control?

8 Payroll system controls

8.1 Control objectives in the payroll system

Setting wages and salaries

Control objective	Risk controlled
Only pay employees for work they have done	Company overpays
Pay employees the correct, authorised gross pay	Company overpays

Recording wages and salaries

Control objective	Risk controlled
Record gross pay, net pay and relevant deductions correctly in the payroll records	Company makes incorrect payments to staff/tax offices Financial statements misstated
Record payments made in the bank and cash records and the general ledger	Financial statements misstated

Paying wages and salaries

Control objective	Risk controlled
Only pay the correct employees	Angry, unpaid workforce Company has to ensure employees are duly paid so pays twice

Deductions

Control objective	Risk controlled
Ensure all deductions have been properly calculated and authorised	Company breaks PAYE law Incorrect pension contributions made
Pay the correct amounts to HMRC	Company breaks PAYE law Company must pay penalties

8.2 Controls in the payroll system

8.2.1 Segregation of duties

Once again, segregation of duties in the system is vital.

Where there is no segregation of duties it would be possible for the person responsible for the payroll system:

- To authorise an inappropriate salary for themselves
- To enter someone who is not an employee onto the payroll.

8.2.2 Control activities

The following are some control activities for specific control objectives.

BPP
LEARNING MEDIA

Setting wages and salaries

Control objective	Control activities
Only pay employees for work they have done	Time at work should be clocked; timesheets should be maintained where appropriate Review and record valid hours at work Review total payroll cost against budget and investigate unexpected variances
Pay employees the correct, authorised gross pay	Maintain standing data accurately Refer to standing data when calculating wages and salaries Engaging employees, setting rates of pay, changing rates of pay, overtime, non-statutory deductions from pay and advances of pay should all be authorised and recorded Record changes in personnel

Recording wages and salaries

Control objective	Control activities
Record gross pay, net pay and relevant deductions correctly in the payroll records	Use wages control account Check and approve amounts before payment
Record payments made in the bank and cash records and the general ledger	Use wages control account Wage cheque for cash payments should be authorised

Paying wages and salaries

Control objective	Control activities
Only pay the correct employees	Cash should be kept securely Identity of staff should be verified before payment Distributions of cash wages should be recorded Bank transfer lists should be prepared and authorised Bank transfer lists should be compared to the payroll

Deductions

Control objective	Control activities
Ensure all deductions have been properly calculated and authorised	Check calculation and authorisation of all deduction
	Maintain separate records for each employee
	Reconcile total pay and deductions in wages control account regularly
Pay the correct amounts to HMRC	Check amounts to returns to HMRC

Activity 7: Payroll system controls

Hinton Ltd has the following controls in its payroll system:

(a)   Changes in personnel should be recorded.

(b)   The wage cheque for cash payments should be authorised.

(c)   Total payroll cost should be compared to budgets.

Required:

What are the objectives of each of the controls?

BPP
LEARNING MEDIA

Chapter summary

- Internal controls in the accounting system aim: to protect it from systemic weaknesses, fraudulent activities and human error; to ensure it complies with applicable laws and regulations; to ensure the company is working to meet its objectives.

- The internal control system consists of: an effective control environment; a robust risk assessment process; appropriate control activities; consistent monitoring of controls.

- Control activities in an accounting system address systemic weaknesses and control risks.

- Control activities consist of: authorisation of transactions; processing controls (IT and arithmetical accuracy controls) accounting controls; reconciliations; physical controls; reviews; documentation of procedures; segregation of duties.

- Application IT controls affect transactions and consist of: input controls; accuracy controls; authorisation checks; processing controls; controls over standing data.

- General IT controls affect the general computer environment.

- Limitations of controls: people make mistakes; controls may not be operated effectively; people may deliberately circumvent controls.

- For each control objective within a sub-system, the risk controlled and control activities need to be identified.

- Within any of the sub-systems, segregation of duties – as far as it is possible given the size of the accounting function and the number of its staff – is a vital control.

- In the credit sales sub-system, control objectives etc are identified for: taking orders and extending credit; despatching and invoicing goods; recording and accounting for sales and returns; receiving payment.

- In the purchases sub-system, control objectives etc are identified for: ordering; receipt of goods and services; accounting; payments.

- In the payroll sub-system, control objectives etc are identified for: setting wages and salaries; recording; payments; deductions.

Keywords

- **Accounting controls:** Examples such as control accounts and trial balances help to identify mistakes in the accounting records.

- **Application controls:** Controls relating to the transactions and standing data in the computerised accounting system.

- **Authorisation of transactions:** A key control activity, indicating to accounting staff that the transaction in question is valid.

- **Control activities:** The policies and procedures that help ensure objectives are carried out.

- **Control environment:** The attitudes, awareness and actions of management and those responsible for ensuring that the internal controls within the company meet that company's needs.

- **Control objective:** The correct action that needs to take place.

- **General IT controls:** Controls (other than application controls) relating to the computer environment.

- **Internal controls:** Procedures that address the risk that the aims and objectives of the company will not be met.

- **Internal control system:** The control environment, the risk assessment process, control activities and monitoring of controls.

- **IT controls:** General controls, or application controls built into the IT system.

- **Physical controls:** Ensuring assets such as inventory and cash are safe.

- **Processing controls:** Arithmetic and bookkeeping checks on whether transactions are accurate and complete.

- **Reconciliations:** Agreeing two different sources of information to highlight if errors have occurred.

- **Reviews:** Looking at summaries and reports of transactions to assess their reasonableness.

- **Risk:** The threat to the company presented by the control objective not being attained.

- **Risk assessment process:** Evaluation of the risks to the achievement of objectives.

- **Segregation of duties:** Making sure that a number of people are involved in different parts of each process to minimise the opportunity for fraud and error.

BPP LEARNING MEDIA

Activity answers

Activity 1: The control environment

A larger company will have a full, documented set of internal controls because many people will be involved in operating them.

A small company will not have many formal controls, since it will have fewer resources and accounting function staff members may have to perform several functions.

In a small company, senior managers may work closely with operational staff and their attitude to controls will be particularly influential.

Activity 2: Risk assessment process

(a) Operating effectively

The business is at risk of not operating properly due to out-of-date machinery.

In addition, the company is facing increased competition from a company which is likely to have more up-to-date equipment and may have a useful knowledge of MEM's operating practices.

(b) Reporting accurately

The qualified accountant is not on the board so this may impair the effectiveness of the board to report properly.

The fact that the company deals in more than one currency increases the risk of errors in the financial statements.

(c) Complying with applicable laws and regulations

The company has a number of employees and must ensure that it satisfies many legal requirements in relation to them.

The company operates from an old building using old machines. It must ensure that it operates within the boundaries of health and safety law as well.

Activity 3: Segregation of duties

(a) There is very little segregation of duties at CCC. Although the key sales, wages and purchase functions are carried out by different staff members, the systems would benefit from some segregation being introduced.

(b) Payments for purchases could be authorised by someone other than Margaret, for instance one of the two Cookridge brothers. It may also be appropriate for the new, full-time, senior accounts clerk to authorise all such payments.

Activity 4: Sales system controls (1)

(a) Credit checks on new customers are to ensure that the customer is a good credit risk and able to pay for goods/services purchased.

(b) Sales invoices should be sequentially numbered to ensure that fictitious sales invoices are not raised (and used to then misappropriate genuine payments for other invoices).

(c) Receivables statements should be prepared regularly to check that the sales ledger has been kept correctly (customers are likely to draw attention to debts that are not genuine) and to encourage trade receivables to pay promptly.

(d) There should be restrictions on who is allowed to receive cash for the business to minimise the risk of cash being stolen or lost.

Activity 5: Sales system controls (2)

Sales orders should be recorded on pre-numbered documents.

Despatch notes should be checked to sales orders prior to despatch.

The sales ledger should be written up more frequently to aid credit control.

The sales ledger should be reviewed frequently to check for irrecoverable debts.

Someone other than Peter should record and bank receipts.

Activity 6: Purchases system controls

(a) The necessity for orders should be evidenced so that goods are only purchased for genuine business reasons.

(b) Supplier invoices should be matched to the goods received note so that goods are only paid for if they have been received.

(c) Supplier statements should be compared to the purchases ledger accounts to discover errors in recording in the ledger and/or to discover whether the company is being charged for genuine liabilities.

(d) Blank cheques should never be signed as signed blank cheques make it easier for cash to be stolen from the company/spent on goods which are not for business use.

Activity 7: Payroll system controls

(a) Changes in personnel should be recorded so that the right employees are paid for work done.

(b) A wage cheque for cash payments to employees should be authorised so that cash is not misappropriated.

(c) Total payroll cost should be compared to budgets because any variances observed might reveal errors in calculation or in payments made to staff or leavers inappropriately.

BPP LEARNING MEDIA

Test your learning

1   **What type of control activity is each of the following actions?**

Action	Type of control activity
Person A matches despatch notes to invoices; Person B creates invoice to customer	Physical control
Control account reconciliation	Management control
Petty cash box kept locked	Arithmetic/bookkeeping check
Adequate resourcing of accounting function	Segregation of duties
Review of budgetary control report	Organisation

2   **Which of the following is an example of an input IT control?**

Check that a sales invoice number has a prefix letter as well as a number value	
Check the number of transactions processed against the number of original documents	
Warning to user not to log out if processing is incomplete	
Regular review of product data to ensure that it is correct	

3   **Complete the following statement:**

Control objectives in relation to taking orders and extending credit are part of the _____ sub-system of the accounting system.

Picklist:

payroll
purchases
sales

4   **Complete the following statement:**

Completion of goods received notes is a control activity related to the control objective of _____.

Picklist:

ensuring goods and services received are used for the company's purposes
recording all money received

only accepting goods and services that have been ordered and appropriately authorised

5 **Complete the following statement:**

Completion of timesheets by employees meets the payroll sub-system's control objective of:

paying employees the correct, authorised gross pay.	
only paying employees for work they have done.	
recording gross pay, net pay and relevant deductions correctly in the payroll records.	
recording payments made in the bank and cash records and the general ledger.	

BPP
LEARNING MEDIA

Analysis of fraud and systemic weaknesses

Learning outcomes

2.2	**Evaluate how information from the organisation's financial statements may indicate weaknesses in its internal controls** • Use ratio analysis • Use key performance indicators
2.3	**Examine ways of preventing and detecting fraud and systemic weaknesses** • The common types of fraud • The common types of systemic weaknesses and their causes • The need for segregation of duties • The financial and non-financial implications for an organisation if fraud occurs • The role of internal controls in preventing fraud and errors • The role of internal controls in detecting fraud and errors
3.3	**Evaluate the risk of fraud arising from weaknesses in the internal control system** • Identify the impact of a poor internal control system on the exposure to risk for an organisation • Grade the risk of fraud using either 'low', 'medium' or 'high' or a numerical grade where the number increases in size as the risk becomes more serious
4.3	**Consider the effects of recommended changes on users of the system** • Identify the changes that users may be required to make to working practices to comply with changes to statutory and organisational requirements • Consider different methods of support that can be given to users of the accounting system to assist them in adapting to the recommended changes

Assessment context

Assessment of these topics will be included within a number of tasks in the synoptic assessment at Level 4.

Qualification context

Ratio analysis and the use of key performance indicators are covered in the other mandatory units at Level 4.

Business context

Every company's accounting system is at risk of fraud and error even if the risks never actually materialise. A company with systemic weaknesses in its accounting system and internal control system is particularly at risk. It can lead to serious losses and fines for the company, criminal prosecutions of those responsible, and ultimately the collapse of the company. Systemic weaknesses, loss and fraud are not uncommon; in Scotland, 14 cases of fraud of over £100,000 were reported in 2014 alone, for example.

BPP
LEARNING MEDIA

Chapter overview

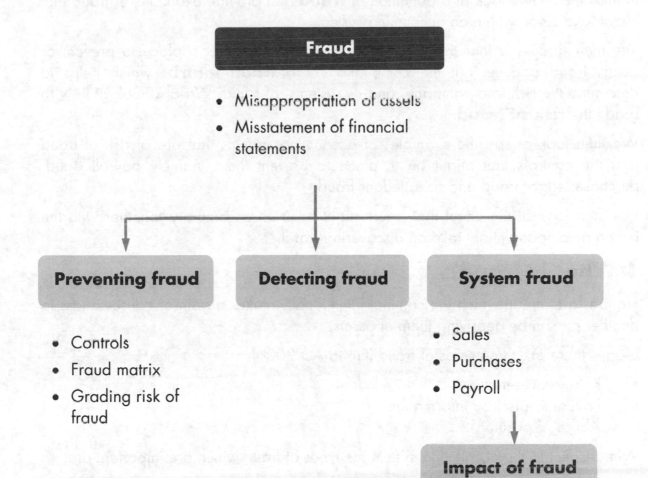

Fraud

- Misappropriation of assets
- Misstatement of financial statements

Preventing fraud

- Controls
- Fraud matrix
- Grading risk of fraud

Detecting fraud

System fraud

- Sales
- Purchases
- Payroll

Impact of fraud

Introduction

In this chapter we look at a definition of **fraud** and provide examples of fraud that might take place within an accounting system.

We then discuss further the general controls that might be in place to prevent or detect fraud and set out the compilation of a **fraud matrix** which helps to determine the risk to a company, and its systems, of fraud. We also look at how to grade the **risk of fraud**.

We then look at specific examples of accounting systems that are at risk of fraud and the controls that might be in place to prevent them, namely payroll fraud, purchase ledger fraud and sales ledger fraud.

We then look at the effect that fraud might have on a company together with the action a company might take on discovering fraud.

1 What is fraud?

Fraud is a crime in which the criminal intentionally makes a gain or causes a loss to another person by depriving them of assets.

Legally there are three types of fraud (Fraud Act 2006):

- False representation
- Failure to disclose information
- Abuse of position

With respect to the accounting system the types of fraud which are important are:

- **Misappropriation of assets**
- **Misstatement of the financial statements**

An accounting system is much more open to fraud if it contains systemic weaknesses that make it easy to misappropriate assets or misstate financial information.

1.1 Misappropriation of assets

In its simplest form, this is the theft of assets such as cash or inventory. However, there is a variety of different and subtle ways in which misappropriation can be accomplished:

- Theft of cash

- Theft of inventory

- Teeming and lading (misallocating receipts to different to disguise the misappropriation of receipts)

- Fictitious employees

- Fictitious suppliers

- Fictitious customers

- Collusion with customers

BPP
LEARNING MEDIA

- Collusion with suppliers
- Receipt of invoices for bogus supply of goods or services
- Disposal of assets without authority

1.2 Misstatement of the financial statements

In this type of fraud the financial statements are deliberately manipulated in order to falsify the position of the company. This could be by:

- Overstating assets or profits
- Understating profits (eg to evade tax), losses or liabilities

Examples of this type of fraud are:

- Overvaluation of inventory at the period end
- Not writing off irrecoverable debts
- Manipulation of accounting estimates to affect profit eg depreciation charges
- Fictitious sales
- Understating expenses

These lists are not exhaustive; you should try to think of any possibilities of fraud in particular systems.

Activity 1: Potential frauds

Read through the CCC scenario at the back of this Course Book.

Required:

Identify the possible frauds that could occur within the accounting system of CCC – even if the controls currently in place make such a fraud unlikely.

BPP
LEARNING MEDIA

2 Controls to prevent fraud and systemic weaknesses

The management of the company have a duty to put in place controls that prevent the types of systemic weakness in an accounting system that opens it up to fraud. The level of controls should be appropriate for the size of the company and the nature of its operations, size and ownership.

Many of the types of internal controls that we looked at in Chapter 4 (SPAMSOAP) are designed to prevent fraud, especially:

- Authorisation
- Segregation of duties – though even if duties are segregated, fraud can still potentially occur because of collusion between the people performing the separate duties
- Reconciliation procedures
- Review procedures

Fraud controls for the accounting system can be grouped into the following categories:

- **Staff controls:**
    - Up-to-date procedures manual
    - Supervision
    - Double checking of calculations
    - Segregation of duties
    - Monitoring relationships within the accounting function to identify the possibility of collusion between staff members undertaking separate duties
    - Good recruiting processes (including the following up of references)
    - Training
    - Membership of professional bodies
- **Management controls:**
    - Up-to-date procedures manual
    - Effective, well-trained managers
    - Authorisation of transactions especially journals
    - Control limits on expenditure and purchases
    - Reporting and investigation of exceptions, eg overdraft exceeded unexpectedly
    - Authorisation levels for activities
    - Internal audit function for monitoring and investigation

BPP
LEARNING MEDIA

- Review of key indicators and reports, eg budgetary control reports identifying the cause of variances; ratio analysis of financial statements

- Support for an ethical culture in the company as a whole and the accounting function in particular

- Support for the key ethical principles among the accounting team of integrity (especially not being associated with misleading information) and objectivity

- **Physical controls:**
  - Keeping and reconciling asset registers
  - Keeping assets under lock and key
  - Access controls to offices and other places of work
  - Signing for wages and petty cash received

- Application and general **computer controls** as discussed in Chapter 4

A key control over both systemic weakness and fraud is for management to prepare a fraud matrix.

2.2 The fraud matrix

A fraud matrix helps the company:

- Investigate the potential for fraud within a system
- Analyse the controls currently in place to prevent fraud
- Grade the potential for fraud, according to risk

Although this is subjective, it enables a risk-based approach to improving controls that are appropriate to the company.

The risk to the company is graded on an appropriate scale:

- 1 = low
- 3 = medium
- 5 = high

Possible improvements to the controls for all high and/or medium risks can then be recommended.

2.3 Identifying the grade of risk

The level of risk of fraud in a particular situation is graded as high, medium or low by identifying two factors:

- The likelihood of the risk occurring
- The impact of that risk on the company

Illustration 1

In looking at the potential for the misappropriation of petty cash in CCC:

- The likelihood is high (5): loose cash is easy to steal and it presents a strong temptation, especially in small amounts as the person stealing it may not perceive the loss to be that 'bad' a thing for the company

- The impact on the company is low (1), as at most the company will only lose £100 at a time.

Combining these two factors, the risk of fraud in relation to petty cash would probably only be medium (3).

Activity 2: Fraud matrix

Refer to the CCC scenario at the end of this Course Book.

Required:

Taking five of the potential frauds analysed in Activity 1 construct a fraud matrix to detail the current controls in place, the grade of risk to CCC, the implications of fraud to the company and recommendations to improve the controls. Ensure the recommendations you make are appropriate to the company.

Potential fraud	Controls currently in place	Risk to CCC 1 = low, 5 = high	Implications	Improvement identified
1				
2				
3				
4				
5				

BPP
LEARNING MEDIA

3 Detecting fraud

Internal controls within the accounting system should be designed not only to address weaknesses and prevent fraud and errors, but also to help detect when they have occurred.

The key controls that detect whether fraud or errors have occurred are:

- **Spot checks** on whether control activities have taken place

- **Performance reviews** and comparisons, especially using:

  - The **budgetary control report**: compare actual results to budgeted results

  - **Ratio analysis**: compare this year to last year, and evaluate the relationships between figures in the financial statements (eg level of receivables compared with level of sales)

- **Reconciliation** of information produced by the accounting system with external evidence, such as bank statements and supplier statements

- **Control account** reconciliations where transactions are recorded in individual accounts and in total (receivables and payables)

4 Sales system fraud

Fraud within the sales system is possible because the system involves the receipt of money, especially where this is in the form of cash, from customers for goods or services sold to them.

Examples of such frauds are:

- **Stolen cash receipts** – cash received is not recorded in the ledgers and is instead taken by employees.

- **Overcharging on sales** – goods sold are overcharged, with employees keeping the additional amount received from customers.

- **Inflating customer orders** – with additional goods being retained by employees for own use or to sell on privately.

- **Writing off debts** – writing off amounts owed and then possibly also keeping any payments made.

- **Raising credit notes** to reduce amounts owed and then keeping part of any payment received.

- **Teeming and lading** – allocating one customer's payment to another in order to balance the books and detract from a shortfall.

Activity 3: Sales system fraud

Consider each of the potential sales system frauds identified above.

Required:

(a) Suggest a suitable control that might reduce the risk of each fraud for a medium-sized company.

(b) What other, more general, examples of controls can you suggest to reduce the risk of sales system fraud?

5 Purchases system fraud

Fraud within the purchases system is possible because the system includes the ability to order goods from suppliers and then to make payments.

Possible examples include:

- **Ordering goods for own use** – and then paying for them through the company's accounts payable.

- **Fictitious suppliers** – making payments to suppliers that do not exist using personal bank accounts to receive the money.

- Paying for genuine goods, but **paying the money into personal bank accounts** instead of paying it to the suppliers.

- **Teeming and lading** – paying payments owed to suppliers into personal bank accounts, then using later payments to pay the original amounts and so on, constantly using funds allocated to alternative suppliers to pay off the earlier debts, with the hope that this will hide that an amount of money owed has not been paid.

One of the key general controls in place to prevent such examples of fraud is segregation of duties: the same member of the accounting team should not be allowed to place orders with suppliers, book in goods received and then process payments to them.

BPP
LEARNING MEDIA

Activity 4: Purchases system fraud

Consider each of the potential purchases system frauds identified above.

Required:

(a) **Suggest a suitable control that might reduce the risk of these frauds for a medium-sized company.**

(b) **What other, more general, examples of controls can you suggest to reduce the risk of purchases system fraud?**

6 Payroll system fraud

There is a risk of fraud within the payroll system because the system involves the payment of money that could be misappropriated.

Examples of such fraud might be:

- **Ghost employees** – having more employees on the payroll than physically exist within the company

- **Overstating overtime pay** – paying for more hours than physically worked

- **Increasing hourly rate/salary** – paying a higher hourly rate or salary than contracted for

- **False expense reimbursement claims** – expenses are often paid through payroll and false claims may be processed this way

- **Retained leavers** – keeping employees on the payroll once they have resigned and amending the bank details so that the pay is paid into own/third party's account

- Unofficially recruiting **new staff** and adding their details to the payroll system

A key general control in place to prevent such frauds is the competence and integrity of the person completing the payroll. This might be strengthened if that person has a payroll or accounting qualification, and is a member of a professional body such as the AAT.

Activity 5: Payroll system fraud

Consider each of the potential payroll frauds identified above.

Required:

(a) **For each one suggest a suitable control that might reduce the risk of fraud for a medium-sized company with two payroll staff.**

(b) **Suggest other, more general, examples of controls to reduce the risk of payroll fraud.**

7 Impact of fraud

Fraud has the following types of impact on a company:

- **Financial** – loss of funds or other assets. This in turn affects the company's profitability and the owner's investment in it. It can also affect the company's share price.

- **Reputation** – exposure of fraud can affect the company's reputation with all internal and external stakeholders. This in turn could lead to a loss of business.

- **Employee morale** – the trust of existing employees could be damaged. Future recruitment and retention of staff might also be affected.

BPP
LEARNING MEDIA

Chapter summary

- Fraud is a crime in which the company suffers loss because someone either misappropriates assets or misstates information in the financial statements.

- Misappropriation can take the form of: theft of assets; teeming and lading of receipts (sales ledger) and payments (purchases ledger); setting up fictitious suppliers, employees or customers; collusion with customers and suppliers; paying for goods and services not received by the company; disposal of assets without authority.

- Misstatement of the financial statements arises from: over- or undervaluing inventory; not writing off irrecoverable debts; manipulating accounting estimates to affect profit; fictitious sales; understating expenses.

- Prevention controls for fraud comprise: authorisation; segregation of duties; reconciliation procedures; review procedures.

- Fraud controls for the accounting system are categorised as staff, management, physical and computer controls.

- A fraud matrix maps potential frauds to the risk to the company and controls over that risk.

- The risk of fraud is graded from low (1) to high (5) on the fraud matrix; more attention is devoted to internal controls over the higher risks.

- Detection controls over fraud comprise: spot checks; performance reviews; reconciliation procedures; control accounts.

- Sales system frauds are typically: stealing cash receipts; overcharging for sales; inflating customer orders; writing off debts; raising credit notes; teeming and lading.

- Purchases system frauds include: ordering goods for own use; paying fictitious suppliers; paying funds into personal bank accounts; teeming and lading.

- Payroll system frauds may involve: ghost employees; overstating overtime pay; unauthorised increases in pay rates; false expense reimbursements; retained leavers.

- Fraud affects the company in terms of: financial loss; reputational damage; poor employee morale.

Keywords

- **Fraud:** A crime in which the criminal intentionally makes a gain or causes a loss to another person by depriving them of assets.

- **Misappropriation of assets:** Theft, teeming and lading, payment of false employees or suppliers.

- **Misstatement of financial statements:** Overstating assets or profit, or understating profit, losses or liabilities.

- **Fraud controls:** Internal controls specifically against fraud in the areas of staff controls, management controls, physical controls and IT controls.

- **Fraud matrix:** A mapping of potential frauds on the company to the risks of each one occurring and the controls over them.

- **Risk of fraud:** The likelihood of the threat occurring and its impact if it does occur.

- **Teeming and lading:** Consistently misallocating payments or receipts within the subsidiary ledgers so misappropriation is hard to detect.

BPP
LEARNING MEDIA

Activity answers

Activity 1: Potential frauds

Frauds that could occur within the accounting system include:

- Theft of assets – computers or other assets could be stolen by any of the staff within CCC due to the easy access to the accounts office.

- Overstatement of wages – there are no controls in place to approve actual wages paid to staff, so the Wages Clerk could overstate wages by either overpaying on hours worked and/or the hourly rate.

- Theft of cash from the office – petty cash is kept in the staff room and there is little control over access to the office. There is no one member of staff responsible for the petty cash tin and the only control is a sheet on which any expenses paid for using petty cash should be logged. However, this control is currently ineffective as it would appear that it is not being used. Staff also have been borrowing money from this tin on occasions. There are frequently discrepancies over the amount that should be in the tin and surprise at finding the tin empty or running low.

- Theft of cheques – there are few controls in place to store the cheque book securely, and it has been found in an unlocked drawer together with blank, signed cheques.

- Overstatement of hours worked – the stores supervisor could add more hours to the staff rotas than physically worked by staff.

- Theft of inventory – there is no mention of controls such as inventory counts to prevent the theft of inventory from the warehouse. The Excel spreadsheet used to record movements of, or changes to the level of, inventory is also an ineffective control as staff fail to update it.

- Overpayment of supplier invoices – there is no control to check that cheques prepared to pay suppliers equate to the amount owed and invoiced.

- Under-recording of goods sold – there are few controls in place to ensure goods purchased are accurately recorded.

- Writing off debts – there are no controls to ensure that debts from customers are not written off, or to ensure that they are written off when they should be.

- Theft of cash or cheques from the mail – no separate controls are in place to record cash and/or cheques received.

- Theft of cash and/or cheques from tills – the tills are not balanced each evening so there is no accountability for any missing cash and/or cheques.

- Theft of cash via the setting up of a ghost employee – there are no controls over the addition of new starters to the payroll system, such as a requirement for documentation that cannot be overridden, segregation of duties, or linking to HR records. This means that a person could set up a fictional employee and keep the wages 'earned' for themselves.

Activity 2: Fraud matrix

This fraud matrix suggests improvements to the controls CCC currently has in place. They have to be appropriate to the company; we could not suggest full segregation of duties within CCC as there are not enough staff working within the accounting function to make this possible! Also the assessment of risk is subjective, based on our knowledge of the company and the controls currently in place.

Potential fraud	Controls currently in place	Risk to CCC 1 = low, 5 = high	Implications	Improvement identified
1. Theft of assets	Physical access to the accounting function controlled by keypad but with common entry code	2	Loss of assets such as computers and possibly key data and information	Access code changed and only key staff have knowledge of it, non-current asset register kept
2. Overstatement of wages – Wages Clerk	None	4	Overpayment of wages to staff	All wages are countersigned on completion and system used to calculate wages based on hourly rates signed off by management
3. Theft of cash from the office	Petty cash is kept in the staff room and office has keypad access Contains notebook for recording expenses charged to petty cash, but this control is often not followed	3	Loss of cash	Door to office should remain locked rather than propped open Petty cash tin should be stored in locked cupboard or safe One member of staff should be responsible for the petty cash

BPP LEARNING MEDIA

Potential fraud	Controls currently in place	Risk to CCC 1 = low, 5 = high	Implications	Improvement identified
4. Theft of cheques	Cheque book kept in locked drawer – but control not always followed	4	Cheques could be used for own purchase/ cash	Cheque book is kept in safe and log of cheques kept to ensure all accounted for
5. Overstatement of hours worked – showroom supervisor	None	3	Overpayment of wages to showroom staff	Staff should sign in and out of work and this should be used for wages calculations and countersigned by showroom supervisor – a more comprehensive control, though perhaps not appropriate to CCC, would be a time keeping system based on staff clocking in and out of work
6. Theft of inventory from warehouse	An Excel spreadsheet showing inventory levels and location of inventory is in place; however, this document is not always updated and inventory checks back to it do not tend to occur.	4	Loss of inventory	Regular inventory checks and perhaps random checks on staff as they leave work

potential fraud	Controls currently in place	Risk to CCC 1 = low, 5 = high	Implications	Improvement identified
7. Overpayment of supplier invoices	None	3	Increased costs	Accounting system should be used that matches invoices to purchase orders and goods received; this will produce reports on total payments for reconciliation Also BACS payments for suppliers
8. Under-recording of goods sold	None	3	Reduced revenue	Accounting system linked to tills could be initiated plus supervisory checks on tills Also inventory checks to identify 'lost' inventory
9. Writing off customer debts	None	3	Increased costs	All debts written off must be authorised by business owner
10. Theft of cash/ cheques from the mail	Cash and cheques received are written into day book	2	Lost cash/ cheques, reduced revenue	Mail opening should be witnessed by an additional staff member Cash and cheques received are double checked by the witness

BPP
LEARNING MEDIA

	Controls currently in place	Risk to CCC 1 = low, 5 = high	Implications	Improvement identified
...ft of cash/ cheques from the tills	None – tills are not reconciled until the following day	3	Lost cash/ cheques	Staff are paid an additional 30 minutes at the end of the day and reconcile their own tills before leaving work
12. Theft of wages arising from the payment to a ghost employee	Documentary evidence should be provided before any new starter can be set up on the payroll system; however, there is evidence that this is not always the case	3	Lost cash/ increased costs	Set up a control in the payroll system to prevent the setting up of a new employee until documentary evidence has been logged Set up a process of checking and authorisation so that a new starter can only be paid once the new starter and the supporting evidence have been checked and authorised by the Senior Accounts Clerk. This should be done via a separate log in to the payroll system Carry our regular checks of the payroll records against the HR system and vice versa

Activity 3: Sales system fraud

(a) Stolen cash receipts – clear procedures, segregation of duties accepting cash payments and recording through the ledgers, good storage of cash and banking.

Overcharging on sales – IT systems such as bar coding that ensure price generated automatically. Authorisation of amendments to prices on system.

Inflating customer orders – segregation of duties and supervisory controls regarding matching orders to goods sent/handed to the customer.

Writing off debts – all debts require management authorisation to be written off.

Credit notes – all credit notes also require management authorisation before they can be processed on the system.

Teeming and lading – regular reconciliations of the sales ledger control account to the balances on the sales ledger; preparation and despatch of customer statements by a person other than the one allocating receipts (segregation of duties)

(b) General controls include:

- Spot checks of invoices to customer discounts
- Authorisation of all customer orders over a certain amount
- Not allowing customers to deal with only one member of staff

Activity 4: Purchases system fraud

(a) Ordering goods for own use – segregation of duties between ordering, booking goods into inventory and payments, plus supervision of each activity including appropriate authorisations.

Fictitious suppliers – management authorisation of all new suppliers added to the system; reconciliation of payments to invoices; also segregation of duties.

Paying amounts into own bank account – authorisation of all amendments to banking details on the system, segregation of duties between amending details and processing payments.

Teeming and lading – reconciling payments made to suppliers and invoices, segregation of duties.

(b) General controls include:

- Authorisation of all purchases orders
- Ordering from approved suppliers only
- Matching of goods received to purchases orders
- Matching of invoices to purchases orders and goods received
- Payments through BACS only and system generated to reflect invoices processed

BPP
LEARNING MEDIA

Activity 5: Payroll system fraud

(a) Ghost employees – reconciling the number of staff on the payroll to physical staff in the company; good controls in connection with adding and removing staff from the payroll system.

Overstating overtime pay – clearly documented overtime rates for staff; management/supervisor authorisation of overtime hours worked.

Increasing hourly rate/salary – clearly documented pay rates; all amendments to the hourly rate on the system should be countersigned by management; segregation of duties so only one of the payroll staff can amend rates, while the other reviews and gets authorisation for this from management.

False expense claims – all receipts included; travel checked for mileage and to diary; all claims authorised by management.

Keeping employees on the payroll – all resignations are officially documented; one member of the payroll staff is responsible for removing them from the system, the other checks this and management countersign.

Unofficial recruitment of new staff – all recruitments have to be officially documented; one member of the payroll staff is responsible for adding staff to the system, the other checks this and management countersigns.

(b) Examples of general controls include:

- Exception reporting – the accounting system produces reports that highlight exceptions to the normal payroll such as particularly high payments, hours worked etc. These are checked and countersigned by management

- Management countersign the payroll staff members' own pay

- Spot checks on payroll staff members' pay to ensure it is accurate in relation to their pay scale and normal hours worked

- No cash payments to staff; all payments by BACS

- Management checks on the payroll reports to look for duplicate bank details, for example

- Rotation of payroll staff across the different duties

1   **Which of the following is a type of fraud covered by the Fraud Act 2006?**

False accounting	
False representation	
Misstatement of the financial statements	
Misappropriation of assets	

2   **Complete the following statement:**

Internal audit activities are a type of _____ over fraud in the accounting system.

Picklist:

application control
management control
physical control
staff control

3   **Which two factors are evaluated to grade the risk of fraud on a fraud matrix?**

Time	
Responsibility	
Likelihood	
Volatility	
Impact	

4   **Complete the following statement:**

Allocating one customer's payment to another in order to balance the books and detract from a shortfall is called _____.

Picklist:

identity fraud
inflation
reconciliation and review
teeming and lading

BPP
LEARNING MEDIA

5 **Complete the following statement:**

The three categories of impact of fraud on a company are:

Morale	
Social	
Reputation	
Environmental	
Financial	

BPP
LEARNING MEDIA

Making changes to systems

Learning outcomes

1.4	**Demonstrate an understanding of the impact of management information requirements on the accounting function** • Why changes may be required to existing systems to meet revised organisation requirements
3.4	**Examine current and planned methods of operating** • Explain that appropriate controls need to be in place during the transition from one system to another
4.1	**Identify changes to the accounting system or parts of the accounting system** • Identify suitable changes to the accounting system • Explain any assumptions made • Identify problems that might occur during transition
4.2	**Analyse the implications of changes to the accounting system** • Quantify the costs of recommendations, stating assumptions made • Undertake a cost benefit analysis • Evaluate the implications of the changes to operating procedures and time spent
4.3	**Consider the effects of recommended changes on users of the system** • Identify the changes that users may be required to make to working practices to comply with changes to statutory and organisational requirements • Consider different methods of support that can be given to users of the accounting system to assist them in adapting to the recommended changes
4.4	**Justify recommended changes to the accounting system** • Effectively present recommendations to management • Provide a clear rationale to support recommendations

Assessment context

Assessment of these topics will be included within a number of tasks in the synoptic assessment at Level 4.

Qualification context

While this chapter draws on costing principles covered at Levels 2 and 3, for the most part its content is new.

Business context

Systemic weaknesses in accounting systems require changes to be made, otherwise the system will fall prey to fraud and error.

BPP
LEARNING MEDIA

Chapter overview

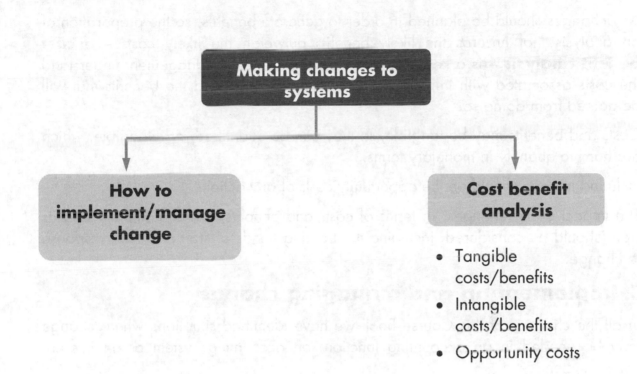

Making changes to systems

How to implement/manage change

Cost benefit analysis

- Tangible costs/benefits
- Intangible costs/benefits
- Opportunity costs

Introduction

This chapter looks at making changes to the accounting system and its internal controls.

Any changes should be planned in order to generate benefits, so the preparation of an analysis that ensures the likely benefits outweigh the likely costs – a **cost benefit analysis** – is a key part of the process. It helps management understand the costs associated with implementing recommendations and the benefits that will be gained from doing so.

Costs and benefits may be tangible, so they can be quantified, or intangible, which are hard to quantify in monetary terms.

Included in costs should be the opportunity costs of any actions.

The impact of the changes, in terms of costs and benefits, on the company and its staff, should be considered, including the training needs of staff and their response to change.

1 Implementing and managing change

In all the chapters of this Course Book we have identified situations where change may be needed in an accounting function, an accounting system or an internal control system.

1.1 Types of change

The degree of change that needs to be made is a combination of:

- The **seriousness of the problem** to be resolved: changing a system riddled with inherent weaknesses or subject to fraud is evidently a much bigger job than ensuring an upgrade of the payroll package proceeds smoothly, for example.

- The **scope of the change**: implementing a complete new accounting system is more of a challenge than revising the responsibilities of two members of staff, for example.

- The **context** in which change takes place: for example calm, well-trained staff will react better to change of any degree or scope than under-trained, overworked individuals.

The degree of change can be classified as:

- **Transformational change** – a wholesale change, eg integrating all accounting functions at a centralised location with a new computer system

- **Incremental change** – a small change or a big change made in small steps eg gradually moving each subsystem on to an integrated accounting package

BPP LEARNING MEDIA

1.2 Resistance to change

Individuals working within a system tend to put up barriers to change (eg objecting, staging a 'go slow', disputing every detail), even when the change is perfectly valid and even when it is quite small. This is because most people fear change, or rather they fear the uncertainty that surrounds change.

Managers need to be aware of this concern, and the resistance people are likely to put up, when planning how and when to make changes.

1.3 Making the change

Steps to make changes to an accounting system:

- Step 1 **Analyse the system and its problems**, and determine that the particular change to resolve these problems is necessary (eg start paying staff by BACS rather than by cash or cheque).

- Step 2 **Choose how to make the change** (eg bring in external contractors to make necessary software changes, or use the internal accounting team to make changes to how existing software is used).

- Step 3 **Prepare a plan for making the change**: this includes identifying who is affected, whether an external resource is needed and what the likely timescales will be.

- Step 4 **Analyse the likely reactions of stakeholders**, not just staff, to the change (eg how will the bank view BACS payments to staff?).

- Step 5 **Draw up a timetable for change**, bearing in mind that:

    - Forced change (eg dismissing an employee who has committed fraud) can be made quickly, but ensuring the system is effective following such a change may take some time.

    - Agreed change normally takes longer, as everyone has to 'buy in' to it, but it becomes effective quicker once the change is made.

- Step 6 **Communicate the plan and its timetable** to relevant stakeholders.

- Step 7 **Make the change**.

- Step 8 **Monitor the effectiveness of the change** in addressing the problem it was intended to remedy, and make further changes if necessary.

2 Cost benefit analysis

A cost benefit analysis takes recommendations for changes and improvements in the accounting system and its controls, and analyses them in terms of the costs and benefits to the company of implementing them.

Change should be cost-effective in that the benefits of the change should outweigh its costs.

Both costs and benefits can be tangible and intangible.

2.1 Tangible costs and benefits

Tangible costs and **tangible benefits** are easy to value in terms of time and/or money.

> **Illustration 1**
>
> The tangible costs of a recommended new computer system are the quantifiable cost of:
>
> - The system itself (training, hardware and software)
> - The loss of staff time while they are training
> - Future licences
> - Future upgrades to maintain speed of processing

Activity 1: Tangible cost of training

A firm of accountants has decided to train all new staff in basic bookkeeping as part of their induction programme.

Required:

(a) **Identify the tangible costs of such a decision.**

(b) **Estimate the costs. (Think of costs not just in terms of money spent but also in relation to time and any other quantifiable measure.)**

BPP LEARNING MEDIA

2.2 Intangible costs and benefits

Intangible costs and **intangible benefits** cannot be quantified in financial terms. (Not to be confused with intangible assets, which can be and are quantified in financial statements.)

Illustration 2

A new computer system may improve the motivation and morale of staff (an intangible benefit) though the automation may mean that some skills are no longer used (an intangible cost).

Being happier, better motivated staff may be more efficient resulting in an increase in productivity; this is difficult to quantify in monetary terms.

Activity 2: Intangible costs of training

Consider the training discussed in Activity 1.

Required:

What would be the intangible costs of the training?

2.3 Benefits

There should be at least some tangible and intangible benefits of suggested changes to the accounting system, otherwise there is not point making them!

It may not be possible to put estimated values to every benefit, especially intangible ones, but describing the benefits clearly is extremely important in a cost benefit analysis. They are often powerful persuaders for implementing a recommendation.

Activity 3: Benefits of training

Consider again the training discussed in Activities 1 and 2.

Required:

What tangible and intangible benefits might there be to such training as part of an induction programme for new staff?

2.4 Opportunity cost

An **opportunity cost** is the value of an activity that has not taken place, because of a decision to do something else.

Wherever possible, the opportunity cost of making a particular change should be included in the cost benefit analysis.

Illustration 3

The firm in the activities so far in this chapter has chosen to send all new staff on a bookkeeping course. One of the costs we have included in our example answers is an opportunity cost: the revenue lost because the new staff are not working for clients and therefore are not generating chargeable hours.

BPP
LEARNING MEDIA

Activity 4: Cost benefit analysis

Consider the CCC scenario at the end of this Course Book.

Required:

Prepare a detailed cost benefit analysis for implementing a centralised, integrated accounting system in CCC, with appropriate staff training.

(**Note** you will not be able to quantify either costs or benefits. However, you should indicate with '£X' within the analysis where a quantified cost or benefit could be determined.)

Chapter summary

- Change may be needed to an accounting system because it contains systemic weaknesses that make it prone to fraud and error.

- The degree of change necessary depends on: the seriousness of the problem; the scope of the change; the context in which the change will take place.

- A change may be transformational or incremental.

- Steps for making a change to the accounting system: analyse the system and its problems; choose how to make the change; prepare a plan for making the change; analyse the likely reactions of stakeholders; draw up a timetable for change; communicate the plan and its timetable; make the change; monitor the effectiveness of the change.

BPP LEARNING MEDIA

Keywords

- **Cost benefit analysis:** Analyses recommendations for change in terms of the costs and benefits to the company of implementing them.

- **Incremental change:** A small change or a big change made in small steps.

- **Intangible benefits:** Benefits of the change that are more difficult to identify and quantify eg improved reputation for efficiency.

- **Intangible costs:** Costs of the change that are more difficult to identify and quantify eg the cost of lost custom as customers go elsewhere during the disruption caused by the change.

- **Tangible benefits:** May be more difficult to quantify than costs, but easy to identify eg less time spent creating invoices.

- **Tangible costs:** Easily identified, quantifiable costs of the change eg buying a new software package.

- **Transformational change:** A wholesale change affecting every part of the system in one go.

Activity 1: Tangible cost of training

Tangible costs associated with training might include:

- Cost of training course – say £500 per employee

- Cost of lost chargeable hours (as the staff will not be working on clients' accounts) – 5 days × 7.5 hours per day = 37.5 hours at a chargeable rate of, say, £50 per hour = £1,875

- Travel expenses to the training provider – say £15 per day × 5 days = £75

Activity 2: Intangible costs of training

Intangible costs might include:

- Other staff discontent as new staff are provided with training they did not have

- Loss of efficiency as new staff's induction is extended and therefore they are not available for client work

- Client dissatisfaction at delays in completion of work due to staff not being available

Activity 3: Benefits of training

Tangible benefits might include:

- Staff being better trained, so chargeable fees could be increased – from £50 to £75 per hour, for example

- Fewer errors in work completed, leading to less supervisor time spent on new staff's work and a reduction in having to amend work completed incorrectly – say 7 hours per week

Intangible benefits might include:

- Staff are better trained in basic knowledge and skills so they are more motivated and efficient

- Staff morale improves as they feel valued due to the investment in training them

- Clients always see well-trained and knowledgeable staff so the company's reputation is enhanced

BPP
LEARNING MEDIA

Activity 4: Cost benefit analysis

8.1.

A cost benefit analysis of the recommendation to implement a centralised, integrated accounting system, and to train staff appropriately on it, has been completed as follows:

8.2. Costs

8.2.1.

An example of a system that would suit CCC's needs is a centralised accounting software package, such as Sage Accounts Professional, which has been specifically created for small to medium-sized businesses. There are many similar packages on the market and a full investigation should be completed to determine which bests suits the company. A reputable, proven package with a multi-user licence would cost approximately £X. The basis for choosing the package should include ease of use (for example drop-down menus), the help facility and the user manuals.

8.2.2.

CCC would also need to purchase an appropriate support package to ensure users have access to trained support professionals and that software upgrades and bug fixes are received. An estimated cost for this is an additional £X per year.

8.2.3.

Appropriate training for staff is required. If the accounting package purchased is one in common use then CCC will be able to purchase places on open courses for staff, costing approximately £X per staff member. CCC might also consider a tailored training course for all staff at once, to include partial set-up of the system for CCC's use, which would cost approximately £X.

8.2.4.

There would be an opportunity cost of the staff attending the training in that they would not be available to complete their work at CCC while they are on the course.

8.2.5.

The company requires the appropriate equipment to network the computers. This could be completed either by cable or on a secure wireless network, and would cost approximately £X. Cabling would be more reliable but would create disruption to the office while being installed, whereas a wireless network would be less disruptive to install but may be less reliable.

8.2.6.

CCC would face some disruption while the new accounting system is installed and set up. There will be a need to pay for additional staff time to enter data for customers, suppliers and employees into the system so that it is fully operational, and it is anticipated that this could be completed within one week. This would require an additional 50 paid hours costing approximately £500.

8.2.7.

A further cost the company should consider, but one that is harder to quantify, is staff discontent at a change to the current system. Staff within the accounting team may be unhappy about needing to learn new working practices, increased controls and how to operate a new system. Other employees may see the increased controls in place as preventing them from carrying out their work, and unnecessary.

8.2.8.

There would be a cost associated with producing procedure manuals to ensure staff know the expected working practices and procedures surrounding the new accounting system. There should also be a rota produced for cover when staff are absent. This should be completed by the Senior Accounts Clerk, as part of their normal role. As an estimate, this would take approximately 20 hours of their time per year.

8.3. Benefits

8.3.1.

The first benefit to CCC would be the ability to produce reports from the centralised accounting system that provide complete information showing the full financial position of the company. These reports can be reviewed on a regular basis by both the directors and the Senior Accounts Clerk. The cash-related reports should help ensure cash flows are effectively managed. This will benefit the company by reducing overdraft fees and avoiding embarrassment with suppliers. The reports produced would include:

- Statement of profit or loss
- Statement of financial position
- Statement of cash flows
- Aged receivable analysis
- Cash flow forecast
- Supplier payment reports
- Costs by cost centre/code
- Analysis of petty cash expenditure
- Payroll reports
- Budgets and budgetary control reports

8.3.2.

An aged receivable analysis can be produced to strengthen the system of chasing overdue debts and ensure customers who have not paid are put on stop quickly. This will prevent customers from taking advantage of the current lax controls. It has been calculated that approximately £X per year of irrecoverable debts would be avoided.

8.3.3.

Cash flow forecasts will enable the directors and the Senior Accounts Clerk to estimate the cash inflows to and outflows from the company, manage cash balances

BPP
LEARNING MEDIA

more effectively and reduce the overdraft and related fees. It will also assist with the planning of any significant cash expenditure. Overdraft fees and interest payments could be reduced by up to £X per year.

8.3.4.

The payroll will be accurately produced when required, with the benefit of the system being up to date on payroll rules and regulations such as tax rates. This will produce a benefit of more accuracy, fewer queries and increased efficiency of staff time. It is estimated that the system will speed up the completion of the payroll by approximately four hours per month.

8.3.5.

There will be less danger from a system breakdown with appropriate backup of a central system. If one computer were to fail then the other staff could continue working, and a support agreement would ensure that if the main system failed it could be operational again as quickly as possible with less risk of lost or corrupted data.

8.3.6.

Another benefit would be improved supplier relations - reports on supplier payments due could be run and suppliers paid on time. This could also benefit the credit terms and conditions that suppliers grant CCC, further improving cash flow.

8.3.7.

Further benefits are the significant reduction in the risk of fraud and the improvement of controls within the system together with improved cost control. Central reports will assist both the owners and the senior accounts clerk with analysing payments and wages, and identifying where costs are higher than expected. Due to current poor controls it is not known if CCC has suffered from fraudulent activities so benefits are hard to evaluate.

8.3.8.

Another benefit is the improved morale of staff. The accounting team would benefit from training, including formal accounting training as requested, and this would improve their efficiency and effectiveness as well as morale. Better motivated staff should result in lower staff turnover and also improved commitment to the company.

8.3.9.

The morale of the non-accounting staff will be improved by the timely completion of accurate wages.

8.3.10.

A final benefit is that CCC will be able to comply with regulations such as the Data Protection Act 1998 with good, secure storage of its data and information.

1 Ard Ltd is a large business with many operating centres. To date its accounting has been done using various software packages on an independent PC at each operating centre. Ard Ltd now plans to move to a centralised accounting function with an integrated accounting system.

Complete the following statement.

Ard Ltd's plan is _____ change.

Picklist:

an incremental
a transformational

2 **Complete the following statement.**

The fact that Ard Ltd's staff in its operating centres will no longer use the skills they have developed in accounting is

a tangible cost of the change.	
an intangible benefit of the change.	
a tangible benefit of the change.	
an intangible cost of the change.	

3 **Complete the following statement.**

The fact that Ard Ltd's employees will be disrupted by the planned change so will not be able to work on an alternative new project is an _____ of the change.

Picklist:

inevitable consequence
intangible benefit
opportunity cost

4 In the process of integrating its accounting system Ard Ltd has discovered some misappropriation of assets and has dismissed the accountant responsible.

Complete the following statement.

This is an example of **(1)**_____ change, and ensuring the system is effective following such a change is likely to take **(2)**_____.

Picklists:

(1) a forced/an agreed
(2) little time/some time

BPP
LEARNING MEDIA

5 **Complete the following statement.**

Change should be _____ in that the benefits of the change should outweigh its costs.

Picklist:

cost-effective
economical
efficient

Test your learning: answers

Chapter 1: Introduction to the organisation

1

Detailed	
Rigid	
Distinctive	✓
For internal publication only	

2   A company with many layers of management can be described as having a (1) **tall** organisation structure with managers having a (2) **narrow** span of control.

3

Goal congruence	
Communication time	✓
Economies of scale	
Standardisation	

4   A bank which has lent money to a company is (1) **an external** stakeholder of the company which is affected (2) **directly** by the company's actions.

5

Parties	Responsibility
Directors	Report whether financial statements show a true and fair view
External auditors	Maintain the accounting system
Accounting function	Prepare financial statements for the company

Chapter 2: The accounting function

1

Budgetary control reports	
Payroll	
Financial statements	
Cash management	✓

2

A centralised accounting function has better communication with business units than a decentralised one.	
A decentralised accounting function has more economies of scale compared with a centralised one.	
A centralised accounting function has more economies of scope than a decentralised one.	✓
A decentralised accounting function is better placed to produce group accounts than a centralised one.	

3   A statement of cash flows shows receipt of a loan as part of **financing activities** and proceeds from the disposal of non-current assets as part of **investing activities**.

4

Receivables days + Inventory days – Payables days	✓
Receivables days + Payables days – Inventory days	
Inventory days + Receivables days + Payables days	
Inventory days – Receivables days – Payables days	

5   The **fixed overheads** total variance may be analysed into expenditure, efficiency and capacity variances.

BPP
LEARNING MEDIA

Chapter 3: Accounting systems

1   An integrated accounting system is (1) **centralised**. One of its core objectives should be (2) **compliance with laws and regulations**.

2

Activities	Type of security control
Validation of input data	Physical access control
Passwords	System control
Archiving	Integrity control

Validation of input data → Integrity control
Passwords → Physical access control
Archiving → System control

3

password	
TekfU4af#	✓
2468TTfn	
The/password@	

4   In SWOT analysis, strengths and weaknesses are **internal to the company** and opportunities and threats are **external to the company**.

5   The requirement for an accountant to act diligently is part of the fundamental principle of

integrity.	
professional competence and due care.	✓
professional behaviour.	
objectivity.	

Chapter 4: Internal control systems

1

Action	Type of control activity
Person A matches despatch notes to invoices; Person B creates invoice to customer	Physical control
Control account reconciliation	Management control
Petty cash box kept locked	Arithmetic/bookkeeping check
Adequate resourcing of accounting function	Segregation of duties
Review of budgetary control report	Organisation

2

Check that a sales invoice number has a prefix letter as well as a number value	
Check the number of transactions processed against the number of original documents	✓
Warning to user not to log out if processing is incomplete	
Regular review of product data to ensure that it is correct	

3   Control objectives in relation to taking orders and extending credit are part of the **sales** sub-system of the accounting system.

4   Completion of goods received notes is a control activity related to the control objective of **only accepting goods and services that have been ordered and appropriately authorised**.

BPP
LEARNING MEDIA

5   Completion of timesheets by employees meets the payroll sub-system's control objective of:

paying employees the correct, authorised gross pay.	
only paying employees for work they have done.	✓
recording gross pay, net pay and relevant deductions correctly in the payroll records.	
recording payments made in the bank and cash records and the general ledger.	

Chapter 5: Analysis of fraud and systemic weaknesses

1

False accounting	
False representation	✓
Misstatement of the financial statements	
Misappropriation of assets	

2 Internal audit activities are a type of **management control** over fraud in the accounting system.

3

Time	
Responsibility	
Likelihood	✓
Volatility	
Impact	✓

4 Allocating one customer's payment to another in order to balance the books and detract from a shortfall is called **teeming and lading**.

5 The three categories of impact of fraud on a company are:

Morale	✓
Social	
Reputation	✓
Environmental	
Financial	✓

BPP
LEARNING MEDIA

Chapter 6: Making changes to systems

1   Ard Ltd's plan is **a transformational** change.

2   The fact that Ard Ltd's staff in its operating centres will no longer use the skills they have developed in accounting is

a tangible cost of the change.	
an intangible benefit of the change.	
a tangible benefit of the change.	
an intangible cost of the change.	✓

3   The fact that Ard Ltd's employees will be disrupted by the planned change so will not be able to work on an alternative new project is **an opportunity cost** of the change.

In the process of integrating its accounting system Ard Ltd has discovered some misappropriation of assets and has dismissed the accountant responsible.

4   This is an example of (1) **a forced change**, and ensuring the system is effective following such a change is likely to take (2) **some time**.

5   Change should be **cost-effective** in that the benefits of the change should outweigh its costs.

BPP
LEARNING MEDIA

Sample Scenario

Cookridge & Cookridge Carpets Ltd

COMPANY HISTORY

Cookridge & Cookridge Carpets Ltd (CCC) is a large carpet, soft furnishings and bed dealership based in Southampton. It is the main dealer for 'Memomemory' foam beds and mattresses in the area, and has been trading for four years. It was set up by two brothers, Peter and John Cookridge.

Peter is a trained carpet filler, and has been in the soft furnishing industry for the past 20 years. Before going into business with his brother he was the Senior Manager in a national carpet chain. His brother John, who is three years younger, was recently made redundant from his role as a mining engineer.

They decided to set up the business using John's £80,000 redundancy money and an inheritance the brothers received upon the death of their uncle. Peter had only a small mortgage on his house, and he managed to raise a loan of £100,000 (using the house as collateral), which was also invested in the business.

The brothers purchased a large plot of land on which they developed a building to use as the carpet and bed showroom. They started out selling carpets, and then expanded into beds and soft furnishings. This expansion was organised by Peter, who had developed excellent working relationships with carpet manufacturers from his time in the industry.

In February 20X3 CCC was asked by Memo Beds to become its main dealership for Southampton, as the existing local dealer was retiring and they wanted a local company to run their franchise. CCC have been very successful in direct sales, and have recently started selling carpets and beds over the internet. This venture seems to have increased business.

Peter is married to Sasha, who is a teacher in the local primary school for children with special needs. They have twin 17-year-old boys, Mark and Matthew, who are both keen amateur rugby players and play for their local rugby club. Mark is at college studying for his A levels, and Matthew has started an apprenticeship in motor engineering in a local garage which is run by a friend of his father. Peter's main hobby, besides watching his sons play rugby at the weekend, is building and racing motorbikes. He is a popular and well-known figure on the local motor racing scene.

John is married to Paula, who acted as company secretary for the first two years of the company's existence. She then left CCC to train as a solicitor.

The business employs 20 staff, composed of:

- 9 direct sales people
- 3 internet sales staff
- 2 cleaners
- 2 car delivery drivers

- 1 accessories sales person
- 3 part-time staff in the small accounting function

You have just been employed as the **senior accounts clerk**, taking over most of Paula's old responsibilities. As the only full-time accounting staff member, you will supervise the running of the accounting function.

The carpet showroom's opening hours are as follows:

- Open seven days a week
- Operates from 9:00am until 9:00pm, Monday to Saturday
- Operates from 10:00am until 4:00pm on Sunday

The accounting function is open from 9:00am until 5:30pm, Monday to Friday.

The accounting function office is located on the first floor of the showroom. Access to the office is by a set of stairs at the rear of the building. Toilet facilities for staff and customers are also on the first floor, so the stairs are used by members of the public.

Once on this floor, access to the accounting function office is easy because the keypad lock is never used – the accounts staff prefer to keep the door propped open. The accounting function office is open plan, with no private working areas.

Both the brothers are key holders for the business. They hold the only full sets of keys, as one of them is always on the premises at close of business to ensure the property is secure. There is an alarm code they set every evening when they lock up.

ACCOUNTING FUNCTION STAFF

The current staff in the accounting function office are:

SONJA DOUGLAS (WAGES CLERK)

Sonja joined eight months ago. She is Paula's cousin, and joined the company when Paula decided to leave CCC. Although Sonja is willing to work some extra hours if required, she does not want to commit herself to any more permanent hours. Sonja gained a qualification in payroll four years ago, but has never progressed any further. She currently works full days on Wednesdays and Thursdays.

STEFAN KALINOWSKI (ACCOUNTS CLERK)

Stefan was employed one year ago. He works four days a week, and has chosen not to work Fridays. This is because his main hobby is music, he plays in a band every weekend and Friday is his rehearsal day. He has had no formal accounting training, but was trained on the job in his last role and by Paula before she left CCC.

MARGARET PETERSON (ACCOUNTS CLERK)

Margaret joined the company 18 months ago (application letter on file but no CV). She is employed on a part-time basis of five half days per week, and she likes to work these together to save on her bus fares to work. She currently works all day Tuesday and Wednesday and a half-day on Thursday morning.

BPP
LEARNING MEDIA

The CVs and job descriptions, as displayed on the following pages, are also in Paula's personnel files.

CURRICULUM VITAE

Name: Sonja Douglas

Address: 24 South Street

SOUTHAMPTON

S12 4RT

Email: Sonja@btinternet.co.uk

Mobile: 07792 236543

Comments: I am a well-organised and competent worker, dedicated to any role I take on.

Education:

20Y4 – AAT NVQ Level 2 in payroll gained at Southampton College

20Y2 – A level maths, grade C; A level general studies, grade A

20Y0 – 6 GCSEs al grade C and above including maths and English

Employment history:

20Y4/5 – Arthur C Clarke (engineering factory) trainee payroll clerk

20Y5/6 – Arthur C Clarke; payroll clerk

20Y7/X0 – Frescos; evening shelf stacker. Reason for leaving: to improve my career prospects

Hobbies: Swimming

References: Mr C Hancock, Managing Director, Arthur C Clarke & Co

Mrs G Biggs, HR Manager, Frescos

JOB DESCRIPTION

WAGES CLERK

Hours: 15 hours over two full days per week

Salary: To be agreed

Responsibilities:

- To prepare weekly and monthly payroll information. To calculate all monies due (wages and commission) accurately

- To prepare payslips and make up pay packets for the weekly paid staff, and prepare Bankers Automated Clearing System (BACS) returns for monthly paid staff

- To prepare all associated returns and documentation

- Must be willing to undertake extra hours as needed

Responsible to: The Company Secretary

Responsible for: Self, security of information and security of payroll cash

As this is a new position, other duties may be required on an *ad hoc* basis.

BPP
LEARNING MEDIA

CURRICULUM VITAE

STEFAN KALINOWSKI

42 St James Avenue
Burnistly
Near Southampton
S25 6RE
30.05.19Z4

Overview

I left the sixth form of Burnistly Grammar School last year, as I wished to enter the world of work rather than go to university, and would like a career in accounting. I am a bright, capable worker, and am happy to work on my own or as part of a team. I was Head Boy at school, and am happy to take on responsibility.

Last position:

20X2–20X3	Accounts Receivable Clerk – Swannage County Supplies (Company went into administration and I was made redundant)

Education:

20Y5–20X2	Burnistly Grammar School	
	GCSE Advanced levels	Accounting, grade A
		Mathematics, grade C
		Music, grade A*

Aim:	To learn more about accounting and to become a qualified accountant.
Hobbies:	Music is a passion, both listening to it and playing. I play in a local group.

References:	Mr J Johnson	Mrs C Smith
	Accountant	Head Teacher
	Johnson & Co	Burnistly Grammar School
	Eastborough	High Road
	Swannage	Burnistly

JOB DESCRIPTION

ACCOUNTS RECEIVABLE CLERK (SALES LEDGER)

Hours: 37.5 hours over five days per week

Responsibilities:

- To prepare sales invoices
- To manage credit accounts
- To ensure that all payments are made within 90 days
- To prepare monthly management information
- Must be willing to undertake extra hours as needed

Responsible to: The Company Secretary

Responsible for: Self, security of information and security of cash

BPP
LEARNING MEDIA

Margaret Peterson
10 Mandela Grove
Southampton
S2 4WS

30.06.20Y2

Dear Sir,

I wish to apply for the position of accounts clerk that was advertised in the Southampton Herald.

I am 57 years old. I have several years' experience in operating accounting systems, but have not worked in this area for over two years. However, though not qualified, I am a competent accounts clerk and references can be obtained from my previous employer, with whom I worked for ten years.

Yours faithfully

M Peterson

M Peterson (Mrs)

JOB DESCRIPTION

ACCOUNTS PAYABLE CLERK (PURCHASE LEDGER)

Hours: 20 hours over five days per week

Responsibilities:

- To check GRN and purchase invoices

- To liaise with carpets, beds and soft furnishing suppliers

- To manage accounts payable accounts

- To ensure that all payments are made accurately and on time

- To prepare monthly management information

- Must be willing to undertake extra hours as needed

Responsible to: The Company Secretary

Responsible for: Self

BPP
LEARNING MEDIA

COOKRIDGE & COOKRIDGE CARPETS LTD (CCC)

MISSION STATEMENT

Our mission is to provide an excellent level of service to all of our customers – whether they are spending £5 or £5,000 – and to provide carpets, beds and soft furnishings that make a house into a home.

We are trying to be a greener company and we recycle wherever possible; we promise to remove all of the packaging from customers' premises, and dispose of this in an environmentally friendly way.

INFORMATION TECHNOLOGY POLICY (JUNE 20X0)

All computers can only be accessed by staff who have been authorised by management to use CCC's computers. All computers must be password protected.

Computers must only be loaded with licensed software owned by the company. No changes to software are permitted without the consent of CCC's directors. No member of staff is allowed to load any software on to computers without prior permission from the management.

No unauthorised devices are to be used for saving, uploading or downloading work (eg discs, memory sticks, external hard drives or other devices) other than those purchased and approved by the company.

Computers should only be used for company business and must not be used to access any social networking site.

Staff making unfavourable comments regarding CCC, their management, operating procedures or customers on any social networking site will be deemed to be guilty of spoiling the reputation of the organisation and this will be a disciplinary matter.

Paula Cookridge
Company Secretary

INFORMATION TECHNOLOGY SYSTEMS

There are four computers in the office, as the brothers have provided one for every member of the accounting function.

These are all run on a stand-alone basis, though they are all linked to the same printer. The inventory information on beds, carpets and soft furnishings is kept on Microsoft Excel spreadsheets. Paula worked with the software previously, and thought it would be a good idea to set up the company accounting system using the same software.

Three computers were purchased new when the company was established in 20Y9 and are running on the Windows 7 operating system; they are also loaded with Microsoft Office 2010 (with a three user licence). In 20X3 another new computer was purchased and loaded with Sage Payroll software to enable the payroll to be run in-house. The Microsoft Office 2010 package was also installed on this new computer.

When the computer system was set up a password was set to protect the information stored on it. The password is 'Paula C', and this is used for everything throughout the company because it was set up by Paula when she was company secretary and has never been changed. The idea was that the password would change every three months by having one keyword per computer and then changing the following number. For example, 'Slug1' would then change to 'Slug2' at the beginning of the next quarter, and three months later to 'Slug3' etc.

Paula had also asked everyone in the accounting function to give their computer a password and send it to her, so that she would be able to access all of the computers at any time. However, this was never done.

BPP
LEARNING MEDIA

ACCOUNTS PAYABLE

CARPETS AND SOFT FURNISHINGS

All inventory is purchased on credit terms from a very wide range of suppliers. This is one of Peter Cookridge's roles, and he enjoys spending time researching new inventory lines and new soft furnishing accessories; he also likes meeting the sales staff from different suppliers. He has a favourite group of suppliers he tends to use, mainly because they are sometimes willing to sponsor his motorbike and racing efforts. There is no formal list of suppliers.

All inventory levels are maintained on the Excel spreadsheets. These have been set up to show:

- Suppliers
- Cost prices
- Selling prices
- Profit margins
- Reorder levels and quantities

Margaret has worked on Excel previously, but this was over ten years ago. While she is competent at inputting data she sometimes struggles with anything beyond this.

Suppliers are paid at the end of the month in which their invoice is received, as long as funds are available. However, some suppliers now request payment within 30 days of the date of invoice, and this is beginning to cause John some concern.

CCC holds a large inventory, with many rolls of carpet in the warehouse for sale on a cash basis. Peter has heard that some large companies have recently asked their suppliers to cut the price by 10% and is considering approaching two of CCC's suppliers to ask them whether this would be a possibility.

All suppliers are paid by cheque. These are completed by Margaret, and then signed by either John or Peter as they are now the only authorised signatories. The cheque book is stored in a locked drawer in Margaret's desk in the accounting function office.

MEMO BEDS

Memo Beds supply all the memory foam mattresses to CCC. These are now the best selling line in mattresses. They supply products to CCC on a line of credit. The showroom mattresses are used as demonstration models, and these are paid for 90 days after receipt.

Customers purchase their beds and mattresses to order. A minimum deposit of 20% must be paid to CCC when the order is placed and the rest of the monies are due for payment by CCC to the suppliers within 60 days.

All inventory records are stored on Excel spreadsheets. It is the job of the Warehouse Manager to update the spreadsheets when inventory is delivered into the warehouse, or when inventory is moved from the warehouse into the showroom. This should always be supported by documentary evidence, for example goods received notes (GRNs).

However, on busy days, the Warehouse Manager will often just update the spreadsheet when sending goods from the warehouse into the showroom, and then ask the sales staff for an inventory requisition note when they are less busy.

BPP LEARNING MEDIA

ACCOUNTS RECEIVABLE

Stefan is responsible for the running of this function. While some customers pay cash for their goods, over 60% take extended credit terms. When Stefan first started at CCC, anyone who applied for a credit account was accepted.

However, Stefan realised that this was not good practice and he now uses a credit reference agency to ensure that potential new credit customers have no history of poor payments. Once the agency has done this check, the customer is automatically granted an unlimited line of credit.

All new credit accounts are set up on the first day of the calendar month. Stefan often works extra hours on this day to ensure this task is completed. All sales orders are received by the showroom store staff for processing, and after completion are passed to the accounting function the next morning, so that Stefan can prepare and record the invoices. Stefan has designed a form in Microsoft Word that he uses as a pro forma for invoicing.

To encourage sales, and to compete with large national retailers, CCC offers monthly payment terms to all customers with six months' interest-free credit. Once this period expires there is an annual interest rate of 28.4%. They finance this through Westbridge Finance, which charges an annual rate of 8.7% to the company.

Stefan is responsible for ensuring payment occurs. The company policy regarding non-payment is as follows:

- Once payment is 7 days overdue Stefan will telephone the customer.

- If payment is not received within 14 days of the telephone call, then Stefan writes to the customer requesting payment and for the account to be brought into order.

- If payment is still not received within the next 14 days, the customer's details are passed onto a debt collection agency which works on behalf of the company.

The debt collection agency charges £80 per case, plus 30% of any monies collected. Though this is their policy, the Cookridge brothers think this is a very expensive option, and often do not bother following through with it.

CASH AND BANKING

Cash in

Stefan opens the mail every morning and sorts through it. Any cash or cheques received from customers are entered manually into a day book to record the receipt. The day book is then used to update the ledger accounts, and the cheques and cash are placed in the office safe until a banking day.

At the end of every day, all cash and cheques are removed from the tills, leaving a float of £100 cash in each till for the start of the next day. The principle is that the till should be balanced to ensure that the cash content is correct.

However, during the week this does not happen as the store closes at 21:00, and the sales staff feel that they should not be asked to do an extra job at this hour.

As a result, it is common practice that all cash (except for the till floats) and cheques are removed and bagged as takings from individual tills before being stored in the safe in the accounting function office.

Banking

Banking is carried out on Monday and Thursday, and this is normally Stefan's job, which he does during his lunch break.

There is often less cash banked on Thursdays. This is because John and Peter have started to take available cash from the office safe to pay wages in order to reduce the amount of money drawn from the bank via cheques.

Authorised signatories

Any one signature from:

- Peter Cookridge
- John Cookridge
- Paula Cookridge (removed from mandate 30.10.X3)

Petty cash

£100 is drawn from the bank every month and placed in a tin. A list of what it is used for is kept in a notebook in the tin, and anyone using the petty cash money is expected to make a note of the date and expense, and sign against this. The tin is kept in the staff room, next to the tea and coffee.

BPP
LEARNING MEDIA

PAYROLL

Until six months ago the payroll was completed by the company's accountants, Southampton Accounting Services. Initially Paula was going to run the payroll, but found that this was too demanding of her time and decided to commission the accountants to perform this task.

However, because the individual hours worked each week by staff (and commissions earned on carpet sales) are so variable, the payroll run is different every week. The accountants charged for the time taken to complete the payroll, so it became a costly process for the company.

The brothers decided that wages and salaries could be run internally. For the first two months they used a temping agency, but this was also an expensive option. When Sonja started working for the company eight months ago, she took over payroll duties.

All staff except those in the accounting function are paid weekly in cash. Pay packets are available from the Showroom Manager, Jim Andrews, from 10:00 on a Friday morning. The rest of the staff are paid monthly, by cheque, on the last working day of each month.

The following table sets out the working hours, rates of pay and frequency of payments for the various categories of staff in the company.

Staff	Rate	Normal time	Time and a half	Double time	Pay period
Sales	£10 per hour	40 hours	Hours over 42 Monday to Saturday	Sunday hours	Weekly
Showroom Manager	£11.50 per hour	40 hours	Hours over 42 Monday to Saturday	Sunday hours	Monthly
General staff	£9 per hour	40 hours	Hours over 42 Monday to Saturday	Sunday hours	Weekly
Accounts	£18,000 pro rata	37.5 hours per week	None – salaried	None – salaried	Monthly

Sales staff earn a commission of 2% on the first £30,000 of sales per month, and 5% on any sales over that figure. John Cookridge is responsible for preparing staff rotas to ensure that there is adequate staff coverage for all opening hours. Most of the sales staff are willing to work overtime, so this does not usually create any problems.

Once the week has finished, the completed rotas are given to Sonja, who uses them to calculate the amount of hours that the individual employees have worked.

Sonja prepares the payslips from this information on a Wednesday, calculating manually any overtime payments due and any Sunday working. From this, she calculates how much cash needs to be drawn from the bank and uses the company cheque book (which is kept locked in Margaret's desk) to prepare a cheque ready for signing.

On a Thursday she prepares the pay packets, which are stored in the office safe for the Showroom Manager to collect and hand out to the staff the following day, though any member of sales staff who is not busy will actually do this. Any pay packets not given out are returned to the office safe and remain there until collected by the relevant member of staff.

Salaried staff are paid monthly on the last working day of the month, and this is done using BACS. The BACS information is prepared by Sonja, signed by either of the brothers, and needs to be with the bank by the 25th of each month.

Envelopes with payslips are handed to each member of the salaried staff by Sonja on the day they are paid. If a staff member is not available, the envelope is placed in their desk drawer. There are no adjustments to be made to any of the monthly paid staff, as overtime payments are not made to them.

Statutory sick pay (SSP) is paid to showroom staff, but the office staff are salaried and are allowed six weeks contractual sick pay per year.

The brothers have always trusted their workforce completely, and there is no requirement, or system in place, for either store or office employees to sign in or out when they start or finish work.

BPP
LEARNING MEDIA

DIARY OF EVENTS

AUGUST 20X2

Peter had taken Wednesday off to take Mark up to London to a university open day. Mark had just finished college, and was going to have that week off before starting as a temporary staff member in the showroom so that he could learn the family business, even though he was more interested in trying to become a professional rugby player.

Sonja was standing at the printer, complaining that yet again the payslips had jammed the mechanism. She was annoyed because the payslips had to be purchased from Sage, and not only were they very expensive, but she only had enough left for this week and next week's payroll run, and she did not want to have to reorder more before she went on holiday.

When Sonja recovered the payslips from the printer, she realised that half of them were now unusable, and so would have to be destroyed. After dropping them in the bin, she asked Stefan to order more before she reprinted the weekly wages run.

Sonja thought it was just bad luck when a message appeared on her computer to show that the printer ink cartridge needed to be replaced. She was further annoyed because she had asked Stefan to replace this yesterday when he was printing out invoices, but he had failed to do this. She threw the empty cartridge in the bin before reminding Stefan that it was only fair for him to change the ink when he saw that it was low. All Sonja wanted was for the day to finish as she was really annoyed with Stefan, and nothing had gone right for her.

Stefan's music was his main love outside of his work. While he was happy to work longer hours than the other accounting staff, he wanted to keep his Fridays free for music. Peter could see no problem with this, so now Stefan worked flexitime, arriving an hour before any of the other accounting staff and departing an hour later to make up his hours so that he did not have to work on Fridays.

As Stefan was the first one in the building on Monday morning, he was opening the post and logging cash and cheques that had arrived into the day book, during which time the telephone rang. It was Margaret to say that she had had a very bad toothache over the weekend, and had an emergency dental appointment for that morning, so she would be late for work. Stefan went back to his task of opening the mail, without noticing he had dropped a cheque he was just about to write into the day book behind the desk.

Paula called into the office before she joined John for lunch. As she was short on cash and did not have time to go to the bank, she helped herself to £40 from the petty cash tin, and told Stefan that John would replace it this afternoon when he returned from their lunch date.

John was concerned that some customers were becoming increasingly slow in making payments on their credit accounts. He asked Stefan to prepare a schedule of receivables, but Stefan was busy doing invoices and asked if this could be done next month. Stefan had not chased up late payments recently because Paula had said that although she was meant to do this on a weekly basis, she only did it when she had time.

SEPTEMBER 20X2

Sonja was going on holiday this month. The last time she went on holiday, she completed two weeks of pay packets on the same date (all based on the hours worked in the week prior to her preparing the wage packets) because she knew that she was the only member of staff who could operate the Sage payroll system. She completed these pay packets and placed them in the safe, informing her supervisors that Stefan would give them out each Friday, and that any over- or underpayments would be adjusted in the following week when she returned to work.

However, there had been mistakes in this process, and it had taken a full month for the resulting errors to be corrected, so Peter had said that she should not do this again. This time, Sonja asked Margaret if she could do the wages run for the weeks of her absence, because she knew that many years ago Margaret used to operate a payroll. Margaret had promised her she would try to do this, but she did not know how to operate Sage. Instead, Margaret said she could prepare the payroll manually using HMRC tax and NI tables, and then Sonja could update the computer system when she came back from holiday.

It was a hot Monday morning and the sales staff complained to Jim Andrews that the milk had gone sour in the refrigerator and they could not have any drinks because of this. Jim sent Kim Lee, a junior member of the sales staff, to the nearby store to buy 2 litres of milk, telling her to take the money out of the petty cash tin. She returned saying there was no money left in the tin, and so Jim took £10 out of the till and put a note in saying what he had done. When Jim complained to Margaret, she said it was strange because £100 had been put into the tin a week before, yet on checking the notebook there was only £40 spent in the last two weeks.

On the second Tuesday of the month, the bank telephoned to warn the company that as they had reached their overdraft limit the bank was unable to honour a direct debit due out that day. John said that this was just an oversight and he would deal with it immediately. He emptied the tills and banked £900 in cash so that the direct debit would be covered. He then asked Stefan to produce an aged receivables list so that he could see why the cash flow was so limited when trade appeared to have picked up. John was disappointed to note that Stefan had not been chasing up debts owed beyond an initial phone call if the customer stated that they would ensure the payments were brought up to date.

Mark was helping Stefan in the office as part of his summer job. Stefan was busy updating invoices and, thinking that Mark had read all the company policies, he let Mark open two new credit accounts for customers. Mark did this, but without taking any credit references.

On returning from holiday, Sonja was approached by Ron Sellers, one of the sales team. He had been expecting commission totalling £80 in his wages, but Margaret had not allowed for this and had only prepared his wages based on basic hours

BPP
LEARNING MEDIA

worked. He told Sonja that he really needed this money, but Sonja knew she could do nothing until the next wages run, and told him so.

Ron was so upset by this that Sonja told him she would borrow the money out of the petty cash tin and replace it when she made his wages up. He was very pleased, and told her that she had made his day, as he had to buy a birthday present for his mother. Sonja was pleased to have helped him, but made a mental note to ask Peter or John if they could provide some training for Margaret so that she could work out the commissions due.

OCTOBER 20X2

A new Warehouse Manager, Joe Bloggins, was employed this month. His last job was at a well-known DIY store, where he was the Deputy Warehouse Manager. The first task he did was to complete an inventory check, and he informed the brothers that there was a shortfall of £3,000 in the actual physical inventory against that on record. He complained to the brothers that there was no evidence of when goods had been taken from the warehouse to the showroom.

Joe also noted that the company they were using to remove waste cardboard and paper was charging per collection, and had started to collect on a weekly basis rather than twice a month as contracted. When he pointed this out to the waste collection company, they informed him that the previous Warehouse Manager had asked for this increase because there was so much packaging to collect. This had been done without informing the management, whom he knew would be happy to accept this as it was an environmental issue. Joe thought that the brothers should contact the new employer of the previous Warehouse Manager to inform them that he should have been given a written warning after making contractual changes without the required authorisation.

Stefan went to John to inform him that there was a major supplier account due to be paid and that the overdraft limit would not allow them to draw this cheque. Stefan had checked the invoice, as it was for nearly three times greater than was normal from this supplier, but all seemed to be in order. John did not know why this had happened, but when he asked Peter why he had placed such a large order, Peter informed him that the supplier had promised to sponsor his next motorcycle show if he increased his order.

Peter thought that this would be good business practice and would help increase trade. When John told him that this supplier could not be paid due to poor cash flow, Peter was very annoyed as he did not want to lose the sponsorship. After having an argument over the amount that had been ordered, John agreed to telephone the bank and explain the situation, and to ask them for an increased overdraft limit for one month only to allow the supplier to be paid.

NOVEMBER 20X2

Once again Sonja was complaining that the printer was jammed with payslips, which had meant her throwing away the spoilt payslips for the monthly paid staff.

She asked Peter if they could have a new printer, or just print the payslips on plain paper, as she did not have time to align the printer and the payslips correctly.

Joe is also a motorbike fanatic, and on the first weekend of the month he went to a motorbike rally with Peter. While there, he told Peter he was settling in well, but was unhappy with the record keeping system for inventory control. Another error had occurred recently when one of the warehouse staff had entered a delivery incorrectly on to the spreadsheet while Joe was on his lunch break. Peter said that as Christmas was approaching they would be very busy, but after Christmas he would review the matter with John and Joe together. The conversation then reverted to the Christmas party, and the subject was never raised again.

Joe Bloggins spoke to Sonja and explained that he had taken on an extra member of staff for the Christmas rush and January sales. He said that the new member would be paid on an hourly rate, and that as he was a student he would not pay tax, and would just need a cash payment weekly. Sonja asked for the new starter document that all new employees had to complete, but Joe had not asked for this to be done, and instead asked Sonja to just add him to the payroll system and he would send through the completed document later on. Sonja agreed, and added new worker A. Lias to the payroll, leaving herself a diary note to ask Joe for the documentation.

DECEMBER 20X2

The first weekend was the office Christmas party, which was held at the Grand Hotel. They had a great time, especially as the brothers had agreed to pay for the evening and had given everyone a £20 allowance for drinks.

Stefan's brother Addie was home from university for the Christmas holidays. Trade was beginning to increase, and January sales were looming. Stefan had mentioned how busy the showroom staff were, and so Addie asked Peter if there were any holiday jobs available, as he could use the extra money to help fund his next year at university. Peter was happy to employ him for the next six weeks – not in the showroom, but in the warehouse.

It was Stefan's role to prepare invoices and send them to customers. He gathered the information by completing day books from the purchase orders which were written out by the sales staff in the showroom. As Stefan did not work on a Friday, he was always very busy on Monday, as he had invoices from both Friday and Saturday to prepare. However, now that Addie was working, Stefan came up with the idea that Addie could write up the day books from the purchase orders, and this would save him time on a Monday morning.

Addie was also into music, and as he had been working on a voluntary project while at university he discussed with Stefan the possibility of doing some type of community event, based on music, to enhance the lives of children at the nearby school for children with severe learning disabilities (where Peter's wife Sasha worked). While Peter thought this was a good idea, John was not too happy about it, and said that if they wanted to do this they would need to arrange it in their own time, and use their holiday entitlement days for it.

BPP
LEARNING MEDIA

Stefan asked Peter and John if he could start college next month to further his AAT studies on a part-time basis. Both of the brothers thought that this was a good idea, and said that while they could not give him any time off to study, they were willing to pay the cost of his course, books and exam fees as long as he guaranteed he would continue to work for them for one year after completing his course. Stefan was happy to do this and signed an agreement to this effect. Peter and John were discussing the importance of training and though they felt that Margaret would not be willing to take it up, they decided to offer Sonja training as well with the same conditions. Sonja was not willing to sign an agreement tying her to the company and said she knew her job and did not need any more training.

Knowing that they were trying to keep receivables more in line with their agreed credit terms, Stefan asked Mark to telephone all customers with outstanding balances. One customer, A. Smith and Jones Ltd, stated that they had paid their account in full by cheque over six weeks ago and were very annoyed that they were now being chased for the money.

CarPet Suppliers, one of CCC's major suppliers, have requested urgent payment of an invoice that has been outstanding for 60 days. This invoice is for £30,000, and though this would normally have been paid, there were not enough funds in the bank to cover this amount. When Margaret informed John of this, he was very surprised at the amount of the invoice, and asked her to review all the GRNs for May to see what carpets had been ordered to cause such a large invoice. Margaret spent a day completing this reconciliation and found that there was an error and they had been charged for 1,000 metres of twisted Wilton instead of 100, this having a wholesale price of £16.99 per metre plus VAT.

JANUARY 20X3

Paula came to the office on a Tuesday. The office was busy as Sonja was on holiday, and Paula was happy to help out by answering the telephone and writing some letters. Paula had just made a coffee and came back to Margaret's desk, which is where she was working, when the phone rang. The caller identified himself as Todd Commins, the boyfriend of Angel, one of the sales staff. He asked to speak to her, but when Paula checked she discovered that Angel was on holiday that week. Todd said it was urgent that he spoke with her, so Paula gave him Angel's home telephone number and address from Sonja's personnel files.

The bill for the Christmas party was received from the Grand Hotel. It averaged out at £160 per head, including all the drinks and wine. John asked Margaret to put the bill through the company accounts by splitting the bill so that £140 was put through as a tax deductible expense and the other £20 per head was put through as a subsistence claim against expenses. However, Margaret knew the bill came to £160 per head, and that as such it was over the limit of £150 for a legitimate taxable expense, and therefore should not be included. While Margaret was aware that the method John was asking her to use to account for this bill would mean a smaller tax liability, she did not like to do this because it was in breach of current

HMRC rules. In the end she did account for the bill by splitting it because she was frightened of what John would say if she did not comply with his wishes.

Peter and John were discussing the possibility of expanding and opening a new showroom in Brighton, about 70 miles away from their current location. They felt that they could run this by just employing one member of staff, managing the new showroom themselves to start with by travelling on a daily basis, and even by asking some of their staff in Southampton to travel across to help out if the Brighton shop got busy. They realised that if they were to do this, they would need to look at the finance options open to them, as they would need to borrow heavily to capitalise this venture.

Peter was very concerned as, although trade had picked up throughout the summer, they were still not trading at the same level as they had been last year. John reassured him, saying that by having two branches trade must increase, and that the only problem was that the accounts for this year would not show such a healthy financial position. However, the company only prepared accounts on an annual basis, and had only ever needed to produce these for HMRC, and therefore he could not prove how this year's trading was actually going. He then suggested that the way to maximise their chances of obtaining the required bank borrowing would be to ask Paula to step in and prepare up-to-date accounts that showed the company in the best possible light by reducing the amount of monies owed to suppliers for accounts payable.

Stefan was annoyed when he discovered that one of the credit accounts Mark had opened for I. Khan had made no payments against credit given at all so far. This customer had bought £1,000 worth of goods and paid an initial deposit in July but had made no payment since then. When Stefan tracked back through the account he realised that no credit reference agency had been used, so he decided to contact the agency to check on this customer, only to find that he had a very poor credit score.

Addie was due to return to university next month. As his printer was not working at home, and he wanted to download and print his timetables, reading list and course information, he came to the office one evening when he knew Stefan would be on his own to use the printer in the accounting function office. Peter was therefore surprised when he walked into the office after returning from a meeting with a supplier to find Addie sat alone at Sonja's computer, using both the computer and the printer. When he asked where Stefan was, Addie replied he had gone into the warehouse because there was a problem with the physical inventory balance not matching up with that on the spreadsheet records.

Mark was tidying up in the office one evening as he waited for his father to come and pick him up. All the staff had gone for the evening, but Peter had promised his son a lift home. He decided to rearrange the furniture and was surprised to discover two cheques behind a desk. One was dated August, and one November. He gave them to his father, who said he did not know where they came from but would bank them the next day.

BPP
LEARNING MEDIA

FEBRUARY 20X3

Mark had decided not to go to university but to enter the family business instead. He decided he was going to work in all areas of the business to gain a full understanding of what was happening, and he would particularly like to look at the purchasing of inventory as he felt this could be managed better.

All the temporary staff were now laid off, and Sonja realised that she still had no information regarding A. Lias, the temporary warehouse worker who Joe Bloggins had employed. She tried ringing the mobile phone number Joe had given her for him, but found the number was unobtainable.

Once again the company had reached its overdraft limit and the wages needed to be paid. Stefan and Mark started to telephone customers with the largest outstanding overdue balances. When ringing one customer, Mr Smythe in South Havant, Mark was surprised when he said he had dropped £500 in cash into the store four weeks ago. Mr Smythe said he had given it to one of the sales staff, and noted that this was a young man, with curly hair, a description that fitted one of the newer sales staff members. Mark went into the store to ask the manager about this cash, and the manager informed him that he knew nothing about it but would make some enquiries. He then organised a search in the store and three hours later called Mark to say that the money had been found in an envelope with Mr Smythe's name on it in the back of a drawer, but that no one could recall it being handed in to them.

Margaret noticed that there was no petty cash left and they needed some money to buy toilet rolls. Peter took £100 out of his pocket and added it to the tin, as that was all the cash he had with him, but again noted that there were no entries in the petty cash book – just several IOUs in the tin.

John and Peter informed the staff that they would be away for the third week in February, as they were going on a family holiday to celebrate their parents' golden wedding anniversary. Peter was concerned that they would be leaving the staff without any financial resources, so he and John both signed a cheque book containing 30 blank cheques so that any bills could be paid if necessary. They gave this into the care of Margaret, who placed it in the top drawer of her desk, and promised it would only be used if necessary.

During this week Ron Sellers came to Sonja and explained that once again the commission he had received was not what he had expected, and he was £65 down. He said he needed this to pay his rent. Sonja didn't think that any mistake had been made, but she said that once again she would advance him, as long as it was repaid from his next commission payment. However, when she went to the petty cash tin, this was empty. She knew, however, that Margaret had a supply of blank cheques, so she used one of these, making it out to cash, and went to the bank to withdraw £100 for petty cash, ensuring she noted the advance to Jo in the petty cash book.

ASSESSMENT TASKS

You have recently been employed as Senior Accounts Clerk for Cookridge & Cookridge Carpets Ltd (CCC). This is a full-time position, and the organisation is willing to support you finishing your AAT Level 4 studies by attending evening classes at a local college.

The first job the directors have asked you to do is to review the accounting system, the effectiveness of its internal controls, and whether the culture of the organisation could be improved in terms of working ethically and environmental sustainability.

You are then asked to make any recommendations for improvements that you feel are necessary. The directors know there are many weaknesses, but are uncertain as to how these should be managed.

To help you in this, they have asked the accounting function staff to prepare some brief information about themselves, an overview of the accounting system, and a list of events that have occurred over the previous few months. This information can be found in the company diary.

Task 1

Analyse the accounting system. You should consider the following areas:

1 **Record keeping systems – the purpose of financial reports, and the suitability of the organisation's current reports to meet organisational needs.**

2 **Internal systems of control – identify how internal control supports the accounting system and the types of internal control in place, and any controls that are missing.**

3 **Fraud – discuss the causes of fraud, common types of fraud, methods used to detect fraud and potential areas for fraud within the organisation.**

4 **Working methods/practices – review the working methods used, including the use of appropriate computer software, and the operating methods in terms of reliability, speed and cost effectiveness.**

5 **Training – identify how training is or can be used to support staff.**

Note: a SWOT analysis is a good starting place.

BPP LEARNING MEDIA

Task 2

Conduct an ethical evaluation of the accounting system

- Evaluate the accounting system against ethical principles by reviewing working practices

- Identify any actual or possible breaches of professional ethics

Task 3

Conduct a sustainability evaluation of the accounting system

- Evaluate the accounting system against sustainability principles by reviewing working practices

- Identify any possible improvements that could be made to improve sustainability

Task 4

Identify weaknesses and make recommendations for improvement

- Evaluate the system to identify significant weaknesses, which should be clearly explained along with their impact upon CCC.

- For every weakness that you identify, make a recommendation to improve the situation.

  - The recommendations should concentrate on the effect that the changes would have both on the organisation and on individual members of staff. They may also highlight training needs or aids to improve staff performance, or changes needed to organisational culture.

- Prepare a cost benefit analysis

  - Prepare a cost benefit analysis for one of your recommendations.

Answer to Task 1: Analysis of the accounting system

Cookridge & Cookridge Carpets Limited

1. Introduction to the organisation

1.1.

CCC is a large, owner-run carpet, soft furnishings and bed dealership in Southampton. It is a limited company, set up four years ago by the directors of the company who employ 17 staff in the stores and one full-time and three part-time staff in a small accounting function.

1.2.

CCC has grown since its set-up as a carpet business and has since expanded into beds and soft furnishings. It has recently brought the completion of the weekly and monthly wages and salaries in-house, where previously this was completed by a third-party organisation. It has also recently employed the fourth member of the accounts team, a Senior Accounts Clerk, a role which includes the managing of the accounts department and the personnel within it.

1.3.

The organisation has a relatively flat structure, as shown by the organisation chart.

1.4.

The accounting system in use is a decentralised system consisting of four stand-alone computers. The inventory control system is based around an Excel spreadsheet and the payroll system is run using Sage Payroll software. A single, simple, predictable password is used widely across the company.

1.5. External regulations affecting the organisation

1.5.1.

The Companies Act 2006 – this sets out the way in which financial statements should be prepared.

1.5.2.

Accounting Standards – International Accounting Standards (IASs) further define the policies and approaches to the preparation of financial statements that the company must take.

1.5.3.

The Data Protection Act 1998 – this regulates how the organisation processes and stores sensitive information on customers, suppliers and employees. CCC will need to ensure its systems are compliant with the Act or risk heavy penalties if data is found to be misused and/or stolen.

BPP
LEARNING MEDIA

1.5.4.

Late payment law – as set out in the Late Payment of Commercial Debt (Interest) Act 1998 the organisation will need to ensure that it does not delay payments to suppliers beyond acceptable periods.

1.5.5.

Health and safety legislation – as set out in a range of legislation, CCC will need to comply with various health and safety principles and policies. These include having nominated and trained first aiders, and safe working practices for staff.

1.6. CCC – key external stakeholders

1.6.1.

Customers – the customers of CCC are individuals who are looking to purchase new carpets, beds or soft furnishings for their home. Their primary concern will be that they are provided with good products and a good service at a reasonable cost. They will also be interested in good credit terms with the organisation. Financial information required will include price lists, as well as information on the credit limit granted to them and also statements regarding how much they owe.

1.6.2.

Suppliers – the main suppliers to CCC will be the manufacturers or wholesalers of the goods it sells on to customers. These goods will include carpets, beds and soft furnishings. Suppliers will be concerned with prompt payment for the goods supplied. Financial information required will include information to enable them to decide whether to provide credit to CCC.

1.6.3.

Bank – CCC's bank is a key stakeholder as the company currently makes heavy use of its overdraft facility. If the overdraft has to be repaid, then this will affect the cash flow of the company and potentially its ability to continue as a going concern. The bank will require CCC's financial statements. In particular, it might request to see an accurate cash flow forecast (cash budget) to enable them to see that the overdraft can be reduced within the timescale set.

1.7. CCC – key internal stakeholders

1.7.1.

The directors – as the owners of the business they will have a key interest in its success and will require various types of information including the financial statements. They will be concerned with the profit of the company, looking at revenue and also costs.

2. The accounting function

2.1.

CCC has an accounting team that is situated on the first floor, above the showroom. There is open access to the floor as it also contains toilets used by customers. There is keypad access to the office itself, using a common code in use throughout the organisation. However, the keypad lock is never used as the accounts staff prefer to keep the door propped open.

2.2.

All staff working within the organisation can access the office and do so to liaise with the accounting team, for example sales staff that wish to query their wages, and the directors to discuss the accounts or to sign cheques.

2.3.

The purpose of the accounting function is to complete all activities relating to the accounting records including the sales and purchase ledgers and payroll. Due to some of the identified weaknesses there is little management accounting activity or cash flow forecasting. An organisation chart is provided in Appendix 1.

2.4. The accounting function – key internal stakeholders

2.4.1

Wages Clerk – responsible for the preparation of the wages and salaries of staff. The clerk works two days per week and has an NVQ 2 in payroll.

2.4.2

Accounts Clerk 1 – the accounts clerk responsible for accounts receivable (sales ledger) runs all trade credit accounts for the company, working full-time hours condensed into four days per week. The clerk has an A level in Accounting but no formal training, and was trained on the job by the previous clerk.

2.4.3

Accounts Clerk 2 – the accounts clerk responsible for accounts payable (purchase ledger) works five half days per week. The clerk has several years' experience in operating accounting systems but this was obtained ten years ago. The clerk is relatively new to this role with CCC.

2.4.4

Senior Accounts Clerk – the recently appointed Senior Accounts Clerk is responsible for managing the accounting team and systems and investigating the weaknesses of the accounting systems, with a focus on the payroll system, and making recommendations for improvement.

BPP
LEARNING MEDIA

2.4.5.

Other staff – CCC staff outside the accounting function – include sales people, cleaners and delivery drivers. CCC's staff are key stakeholders of the accounting function. They are primarily interested in good working conditions and pay. They need to be paid the correct amount, on time. This requires an efficient, adequately controlled payroll system. Other staff also require accurate inventory information from the accounting team.

3. Review of the accounting system

3.1.

This review analyses the accounting system in place within CCC and makes recommendations to improve it.

3.2.

The weaknesses have been identified with the aid of a SWOT analysis – see Appendix 2. This review documents an investigation of the system and considers the information the accounting system should provide to stakeholders. It also considers whether the system is suitable to meet stakeholder needs and the organisation's needs.

3.3. Working methods and practices

3.3.1.

The IT systems in CCC's accounting function consist of four stand-alone computers, each operating independently of each other. The accounting and Inventory system uses spreadsheet software (Excel), and the payroll system uses Sage Payroll. Invoices to customers are completed using word processing software (Word).

3.3.2.

Computer files are password protected, although the same – very weak – password is used across the company.

3.3.3.

Weaknesses in the working methods and practices within the systems at CCC are detailed in the SWOT analysis in Appendix 2. The main points from this are:

- There is a lack of communication. Most staff are part-time and some rarely see each other. This lack of communication can lead to inefficiencies if they are trying to complete each other's work.

- The separate, independent systems have contributed to the lack of cover across roles within the company.

- There is no centralised reporting due to the separate systems in use – this has led to an incomplete picture of the financial position of the company, especially in relation to cash flow.

- Many of the current working methods are manual, even more so if a staff member is absent and another person steps in. This could lead to errors.

- The current systems are slow for staff to use. Also, some staff are not fully trained, so are inefficient. The use of Excel and Word provides flexibility, but the lack of controls in these general-purpose software applications increases the potential for errors.

- There is no backup taken of the system, putting the organisation at risk of losing key data if the systems fail.

- There is a lack of work planning, which could lead to inefficient working, bottlenecks, errors and inconsistencies.

3.4. Record keeping systems

3.4.1.

Weaknesses in the record keeping system are identified as part of the SWOT analysis in Appendix 2. The main points include:

- There is no cover for staff when absent leading to urgent work being completed manually and computerised records not being updated.

- Gross pay is calculated manually, which increases the risk of errors.

- A reliance on Excel and Word for record keeping, especially by untrained staff, can lead to errors and inefficiencies. Few staff have the Excel skills required. Errors built into the spreadsheet could go unnoticed.

- Petty cash is not recorded correctly and cash is taken from tills.

- When the tills are closed at the end of the day there is no recording of balances of cash/cheques etc.

- Wages have been completed in advance and therefore were not accurate.

- Errors in wages have been corrected via a cash advance borrowed from the petty cash tin.

- Cheque use is not recorded; there are incomplete records as to what they have been used for.

3.5. Training

3.5.1.

The SWOT analysis in Appendix 2 analyses the weaknesses within the system with regard to training. The main points include:

- Staff lack accounting knowledge and training. As a result, there are inadequate general controls and procedures, and a lack of responsibility taken for their work.

- Staff have not received training in the systems used, for example in Excel. This increases the risk of error.

BPP
LEARNING MEDIA

- Staff have not been made aware of the ethical principles to which the business should adhere (see Appendix 4). One example is the failure to maintain confidentiality.

- Staff have not been made aware of the importance of sustainability in the operations of the business. Ink cartridges are not recycled and paper is wasted.

Answer to Task 2: Ethical evaluation of the accounting system

An ethical review of the accounting system identifying potential breaches and recommending best practice is shown in Appendix 4. In summary, the issues include:

(a) Personal details of a member of staff have been given out without the permission of the employee, a breach of the ethical principle of confidentiality and of data protection law.

(b) HMRC tax regulations have been breached by splitting payments to get around tax deductible expense limits.

(c) Misleading accounts have been prepared in order to secure a bank loan – a dishonest, unethical and fraudulent action.

(d) The company has a Microsoft Office user licence for three users; however, this is used by four users.

Answer to Task 3: Sustainability review of the accounting system

Appendix 5 is a sustainability review of the accounting system. It finds that:

(a) CCC addresses environmental issues in its mission statement. However, this statement needs to be backed up by policies and procedures that are implemented at operational level.

(b) Ink cartridges are currently not recycled.

(c) Paper (particularly payslip paper) is wasted.

Answer to Task 4: Internal control and analysis of fraud

4.1. Internal systems of control

4.1.1.

Within CCC controls are very informal. Reliance is often based on trust. Formal internal controls would support the accounting system and reduce the possibility of fraud occurring.

4.1.2.

The SWOT analysis in Appendix 2 analyses the internal control and fraud weaknesses. The main points are:

- Cash – there are few controls regarding the use of cash within the company. The contents of tills are not counted, cash from tills and the petty cash tin is used to pay wages; there is no double check of the wages when completed.

- Cheques – controls are inadequate and ineffective. The desk drawer where the cheque book is kept has been found unlocked. Blank cheques are also signed and left with staff.

- Authorisation – there are no authorisation procedures in place. All cheques have to be signed by one of the directors – as a consequence blank signed cheques are left when the directors are absent. Wages are not authorised effectively and are calculated from unchecked staff rotas.

- Counter-signatures – cash wages are not double checked and countersigned to prevent errors/fraud.

- Passwords/access – one simple, common password is used throughout the company including for access to the accounting function office and systems. Any member of staff could use this password.

- Credit control – the only current control in respect of granting credit to customers is to check with a credit reference agency; however, it was found that in some cases even this was not done.

- New suppliers/customers – there are no controls in place before new suppliers and customers are added to the systems.

- Amendments to contracts with existing suppliers – there are no controls or authorisation processes in place for the amendment of existing contracts.

- Petty cash – no control system is in place.

- Debt recovery – while a relationship with a debt collection agency is in place, this is rarely used due to the costs involved. The debt collection procedures beyond an initial phone call are also often not followed. This may mean that debts are never recovered.

BPP
LEARNING MEDIA

4.2. Analysis of fraud

4.2.1.

There are many possible frauds that could occur within the system at CCC, and appropriate controls should be in place to prevent them.

4.2.2.

The SWOT analysis in Appendix 2 identifies the weaknesses with the system that open it up to fraud and other illegalities as follows:

- The use of cash to pay wages could lead to the theft of cash.

- The use of cash to pay wages could lead to the payroll staff colluding with weekly staff and adding more cash to the pay packet than the amount earned or shown on the wages slip.

- Cheques are not stored securely, so could be stolen and used fraudulently.

- Cheques are signed and left blank for staff to use when the owner is absent. This increases the risk of fraudulent use.

- There are no controls on new suppliers so staff could defraud the company by setting up a bogus supplier and making payments to it.

- There are no controls on new customers so staff could defraud the company by setting up a bogus customer.

- There are no controls over the setting up of new employees, which could lead to the setting up of ghost employees for personal gain.

4.2.3.

Each of these potential frauds, the current controls in place and the recommendations to improve can be found within a fraud matrix in Appendix 3. This matrix also indicates the level of risk to the organisation.

4.3. Recommendations to improve

There are many recommendations that can be implemented to address the weaknesses identified above and in Appendix 2.

A centralised, integrated accounting software package should be implemented. This will require the computers currently in use within the accounting function to be networked, so all staff access the same files. This would enable the company to have central, integrated accounting records. Staff morale and motivation should improve, as they will be learning new skills, using an effective system and be provided with appropriate information. The reduction in manual calculations would lead to fewer errors, benefiting staff and the company.

Staff must be fully trained to use the new accounting system so they can operate it effectively and efficiently. This will improve their productivity and morale.

The system should also be properly backed up with procedures detailing who is responsible for completing this at the end of each working day. This will ensure the company does not lose key information in the event of a system failure.

Staff should receive formal accounting training. This will show them they are valued, make them more effective, motivate them and provide them with a much better understanding of the need for appropriate controls. This will in turn benefit the company.

There should also be a review of staff hours and days to ensure that staff are in the office at appropriate times, plus there should be a formal procedure in place to train staff in second roles to cover absences. This will improve morale, as staff are better trained and have more variety in their work, and benefit CCC as there will be appropriate cover in place.

This could be strengthened by the completion of procedural manuals to explain how to operate the systems. This will aid the accounting function in the event that training new staff is required.

The accounting function office door must be kept closed at all times and an effective access code used. All staff must be informed of the need to control access to the office. This will reduce the risk of unauthorised access and fraud.

Passwords to access the accounting system must be robust and changed regularly. Passwords should:

- Not contain the name of any user or use numbers or special characters to get around this

- Be at least eight characters long

- Contain at least one number, one uppercase letter, one lowercase letter and one special character (eg @#%)

- Be changed regularly

The controls should prevent the re-use of any password that has been used within the last year.

This will reduce the risk of unauthorised access and fraud.

As part of the centralised accounting system, use of the BACS payments system should be expanded so that suppliers and staff wages are paid direct into bank accounts, reducing the use of cash and cheques. This will significantly reduce the risk of fraud together with the risk of theft of cash and errors in calculations.

An effective petty cash system should be implemented and petty cash recorded appropriately. This will benefit the company by reducing the risk of theft and of inadequate record keeping, for example cash taken from the tills.

The contents of all tills must be counted and reconciled at the end of each working day – staff should be paid to stay back and complete this vital work. This will reduce the risk of fraud and of errors, and make showroom staff more accountable

BPP LEARNING MEDIA

for the contents of their till. The culture must move towards one of controls and accountability.

There should be controls in place for adding new suppliers and customers to the accounting system, with authorisation only from a director and/or the Senior Accounts Clerk.

The cheque book should be kept locked in a safe and the system of signing blank cheques stopped. The Senior Accounts Clerk could be added as a second signatory if required. This will ensure staff are happy that they can have cheques authorised in the event of the directors' absence and benefit CCC by reducing the risk of fraud.

Further checks on customers should be completed before they are granted credit. This will benefit the company by reducing the risk of irrecoverable debts and ensuring that credit is only granted to customers who are likely to be able to pay their debts.

The centralised accounting system will enable full financial statements, budgetary control reports and cash forecasts to be produced, enabling both the directors and the Senior Accounts Clerk to review all aspects of the company's financial position. This will ensure better planning of cash flows so that the current overdraft can be reduced and aged receivables dealt with appropriately. It will also ensure that suppliers are paid promptly. This will reduce the risk of CCC violating their agreed credit terms and being placed on 'stop' due to unpaid bills.

New employees should only be set up on the payroll system upon receipt of specified documentary evidence. It should not be possible to override this requirement. An authorisation procedure should also be required to change the details of existing employees.

The Senior Accounts Clerk should be responsible for the operation and management of the new accounting system, including the setting of appropriate password controls.

A process for checking and authorisation should be set up to ensure that a new starter can only be paid following authorisation from the Senior Accounts Clerk. This should be done via a separate login to the payroll system.

Regular checks should be carried out of the payroll records against the HR records and vice versa.

A list of preferred suppliers should be established. Selection should be based on commercial criteria including price, reliability and quality.

A formal tender process should be set up for large contracts.

When sourcing new items for which there is no existing approved supplier a minimum of three quotes should be obtained. The company that provides the best value for money, taking into account price, quality and other relevant factors, should be selected (this may not necessarily be the cheapest potential supplier, although it may be).

4.4 Cost benefit analysis

A cost benefit analysis of the recommendation to implement a centralised accounting system, and train staff appropriately on it, has been completed as follows:

4.4.1 Costs

An example of a system that would suit CCC's needs is a centralised accounting software package, such as Sage Accounts Professional, which has been specifically created for small to medium-sized businesses. There are many similar packages on the market and a full investigation should be completed to determine which bests suits the company. A reputable, proven package with a multi-user licence would cost approximately £X. The basis for choosing the package should include ease of use (for example drop-down menus), the help facility and the user manuals.

CCC would also need to purchase an appropriate support package to ensure users have access to trained support professionals and that software upgrades and bug fixes are received. An estimated cost for this is an additional £X per year.

Appropriate training for staff is required. If the accounting package purchased is one in common use then CCC will be able to purchase places on open courses for staff, costing approximately £X per staff member. CCC might also consider a tailored training course for all staff at once, to include partial set up of the system for CCC's use, which would cost approximately £X.

There would be an opportunity cost of the staff attending the training in that they would not be available to complete their work at CCC while they are on the course.

The company requires the appropriate equipment to network the computers. This could be completed either by cable or on a secure wireless network, and would cost approximately £X. Cabling would be more reliable but would create disruption to the office while being installed, whereas a wireless network would be less disruptive to install but may be less reliable.

CCC would face some disruption while the new accounting system is installed and set up. There will be a need to pay for additional staff time to enter data for customers, suppliers and employees into the system so that it is fully operational, and it is anticipated that this could be completed within one week. This would require an additional 50 paid hours costing approximately £500.

A further cost the company should consider, but one that is harder to quantify, is staff discontent at a change to the current system. Staff within the accounting team may be unhappy about needing to learn new working practices, increased controls and how to operate a new system. Other employees may see the increased controls in place as preventing them carrying out their work, and unnecessary.

There would be a cost associated with producing procedure manuals to ensure staff know the expected working practices and procedures surrounding the new accounting system. There should also be a rota produced for cover when staff are absent. This should be completed by the Senior Accounts Clerk, as part of their

BPP
LEARNING MEDIA

normal role. As an estimate, this would take approximately 20 hours of their time per year.

4.4.2 Benefits

The first benefit to CCC would be the ability to produce reports from the centralised accounting system that provide complete information showing the full financial position of the company. These reports can be reviewed on a regular basis by both the directors and the Senior Accounts Clerk. The cash-related reports should help ensure cash flows are effectively managed. This will benefit the company by reducing overdraft fees and avoiding embarrassment with suppliers. The reports produced would include:

- Statement of profit or loss
- Statement of financial position
- Statement of cash flows
- Aged receivable analysis
- Cash flow forecast
- Supplier payment reports
- Costs by cost centre/code
- Analysis of petty cash expenditure
- Payroll reports
- Budgets and budgetary control reports

An aged receivable analysis can be produced to strengthen the system of chasing overdue debts and ensure customers who have not paid are put on stop quickly. This will prevent customers from taking advantage of the current lax controls. It has been calculated that approximately £X per year of irrecoverable debts would be avoided.

Cash flow forecasts will enable the directors and the Senior Accounts Clerk to estimate the cash inflows to and outflows from the organisation, manage cash balances more effectively and reduce the overdraft and related fees. It will also assist with the planning of any significant cash expenditure. Overdraft fees and interest payments could be reduced by up to £X per year.

The payroll will be accurately produced when required, with the benefit of the system being up to date on payroll rules and regulations such as tax rates. This will produce a benefit of more accuracy, fewer queries and increased efficiency of staff time. It is estimated that the system will speed up the completion of the payroll by approximately four hours per month.

There will be less danger from a system breakdown with appropriate backup of a central system. If one computer were to fail then the other staff could continue working, and a support agreement would ensure that if the main system failed it could be operational again as quickly as possible with less risk of lost or corrupted data.

Another benefit would be improved supplier relations – reports on supplier payments due could be run and suppliers paid on time. This could also benefit the credit terms and conditions that suppliers grant CCC, further improving cash flow.

Further benefits are the significant reduction in the risk of fraud and the improvement of controls within the system together with improved cost control. Central reports will assist both the owners and the Senior Accounts Clerk with analysing payments and wages and identifying where costs are higher than expected. Due to current poor controls it is not known if CCC has suffered from fraudulent activities so benefits are hard to evaluate.

A benefit would also be improved morale of staff. The accounting team would benefit from training, including formal accounting training as requested, and this would improve their efficiency and effectiveness as well as morale. Better motivated staff should result in lower staff turnover and also improved commitment to the company.

The morale of the non-accounting staff would be improved by the timely completion of accurate wages.

A final benefit would be that CCC would be able to comply with regulations such as the Data Protection Act 1998 with good, secure storage of its data and information.

BPP
LEARNING MEDIA

Appendix 1 – Organisation Chart

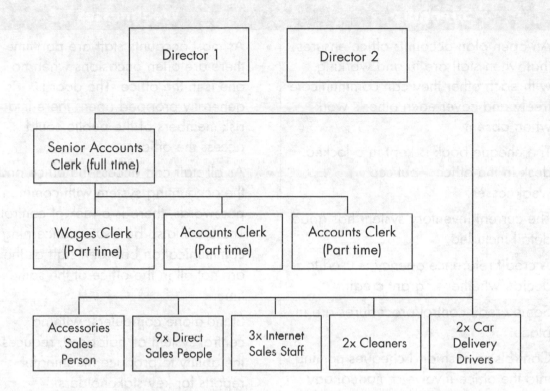

```
        ┌─────────────┐        ┌─────────────┐
        │  Director 1  │        │  Director 2  │
        └─────────────┘        └─────────────┘

┌──────────────────┐
│ Senior Accounts  │
│ Clerk (full tIme)│
└──────────────────┘

┌──────────────┐   ┌──────────────┐   ┌──────────────┐
│ Wages Clerk  │   │Accounts Clerk│   │Accounts Clerk│
│ (Part time)  │   │ (Part time)  │   │ (Part time)  │
└──────────────┘   └──────────────┘   └──────────────┘

┌───────────┐ ┌──────────┐ ┌──────────┐ ┌──────────┐ ┌──────────┐
│Accessories│ │9x Direct │ │3x Internet│ │2x Cleaners│ │  2x Car  │
│  Sales    │ │Sales     │ │Sales Staff│ │          │ │ Delivery │
│  Person   │ │People    │ │          │ │          │ │  Drivers │
└───────────┘ └──────────┘ └──────────┘ └──────────┘ └──────────┘
```

Appendix 2 – SWOT analysis

Strengths	Weaknesses
• An open plan accounts office ensures that when staff are in and working with each other they can communicate freely and cover each other's work when absent.	• As most accounts staff are part-time there are often occasions when no one is in the office. The door is generally propped open; there is a risk members of the public could access the office.
• The cheque book is kept in a locked desk in the office – but see weaknesses.	• As all staff can access the office and the accounting system with common passwords, there is a lack of control. There will also be issues concerning communication between staff as they are not all in the office at the same time.
• The current inventory system has good detail included.	
• A credit reference agency is used to decide whether to grant credit.	
• Some credit control procedures are in place.	• Stand-alone computers, with no central system or database, reduces the ability to produce meaningful reports for key stakeholders.
• Controls re cash and cheques coming into the office involve a manual day book then accounts.	• Staff, as a whole, are not qualified in accounting, which poses a risk of errors and relaxed controls and also a lack of accountability.
• Staff seem keen to improve systems – the Accounts Receivable Clerk has implemented some initiatives.	• There appears to be a lack of planning in the work of the accounting team, highlighted by the fact that when the payroll was first brought in-house a temping agency was contracted to run it for the first two months. This could have led to errors and inconsistencies in the work and the handover of the system to the Wages Clerk once employed.
• Cash movement is reduced by using cash to make up wages.	
	• Stores staff are paid in cash which poses a risk of theft.
	• Office staff are paid by cheque – the frequent use of cheques can lead to the risk of cheques being stolen and fraudulently used.
	• Manual calculation of weekly payroll with no secondary check is a weakness as it can lead to errors or fraudulent increases in staff pay.

BPP LEARNING MEDIA

Strengths	Weaknesses
	• Wages are paid in cash – any use of cash poses a risk of theft.
	• Overdue debts are often not followed up beyond an initial phone call.
	• The cheque book is kept in an easily accessible drawer which is sometimes left unlocked.
	• Staff are not trained in Excel, increasing the risk of errors.
	• New credit customers are not given a realistic credit limit.
	• Invoices are produced using Word – this has potential for errors.
	• Cash is not counted when removed from the tills on weekdays.
	• No controls over petty cash and over cash taken from tills.
	• No contingency planning – accounting staff are not able to take on each other's roles when absent.
	• Staff are unable to cover each other's roles as they lack the skills to do so.
	• No control on authorisation – signing of blank cheques to cover absence.
	• No controls on payments to suppliers or payments from customers.
	• Payments to suppliers are made without checking systems or informing other staff.
	• Lack of controls on staff hours have led to incorrect rotas and staff pay.
	• Pay packets for more than one pay period can be completed in one go – this is a weakness as too much cash was in the office.
	• Wages should be completed correctly each week, not in advance and adjusted later.

Opportunities	Threats
• There is an opportunity to use one central accounting system on networked computers, which will ensure there is better cover for work when staff are absent and better reporting of key financial information to relevant stakeholders.	• Using spreadsheet software (Excel) to prepare accounts poses a risk of errors being made in formulas that are difficult to spot, resulting in incorrect inventory and accounting information.
• There is an opportunity to train staff in accounting and also in the systems they use, making them much more aware of the controls and procedures they should be operating and also more efficient.	• The use of one common password is a threat to systems and the data held within them (for example through unauthorised access).
• There is an opportunity to train staff in each other's roles – perhaps with a backup member of staff for each. This could motivate staff and also ensure cover during absence.	• The lack of formal procedures and controls has contributed to extensive use of the overdraft facility and caused the bank concern. This is a cash flow threat to the company.
• There is an opportunity to outsource the payroll function to the company accountants.	• There appears to be no backup taken of the current systems. This is a threat because key financial data would be lost if the systems failed.
	• Regulatory environment – this is constantly changing, for example potential changes to VAT rates. The accounting system needs to be able to recognise these changes and react accordingly.
	• Debt collection – while a relationship with a debt collection agency is in place, this is rarely used due to the costs involved. This may mean that debts are never recovered.

BPP
LEARNING MEDIA

Appendix 3 – Fraud Matrix

Potential fraud	Current control	Risk to the organisation	Recommendation
The use of cash to pay wages could lead to the theft of cash.	Cash is kept in the safe.	5 – High	Pay staff by BACS, reducing the use of cash.
The use of cash to pay wages could lead to the payroll staff colluding with weekly staff and adding more cash to the pay packet than earned and changing the wages slip.	None – wages are not double checked or countersigned.	5 – High	Either ensure a thorough check of wages calculated and cash included or pay staff by BACS as above.
Cheques are not stored securely, so could be stolen and used fraudulently.	Cheques are stored in a locked drawer – but this is often found to be unlocked.	4 – High	Store cheques in the safe only.
Cheques are signed and left blank for staff to use when the owners are absent. This increases the risk of fraudulent use.	None	5 – High	Allow a second signatory for when owners are absent and reduce use of cheques through BACS wages and payments.
There are no controls re new suppliers and so staff could defraud the company by setting up a bogus supplier and making payments to it.	None	3 – Medium	All new suppliers and customers should be entered to a central accounting system and authorised either by the owners or the Senior Accounts Clerk.
There are no controls over the setting up of new employees, which could lead to the setting up of ghost employees for personal gain.	Documentary evidence should be received but the system does not enforce this.	4 – High	New employees should only be set up on the system upon receipt of documentary evidence. It should not be possible to override this requirement. Set up a process of checking and

Potential fraud	Current control	Risk to the organisation	Recommendation
			authorisation so that a new starter can only be paid once they and the supporting evidence have been checked and authorised by the Senior Accounts Clerk. This should be done via a separate log in to the payroll system.
			Carry out regular checks of the payroll records against the HR system and vice versa.

Key to risk

1 = Low, 3 = Medium, 5 = High

BPP LEARNING MEDIA

Appendix 4 – Ethical review of the accounting system

Current practice	Principle breached and details	Recommended practice
Disclosure of personal details (address and telephone number) of a member of staff to an individual on the telephone.	CONFIDENTIALITY The law requires accountants to respect the confidentiality of information acquired as a result of professional and business relationships and not disclose such information to third parties without proper and specific authority unless there is a legal or professional right or duty to disclose.	Personal details of staff should be stored in accordance with the Data Protection Act and not disclosed without the permission of the employee in question, or unless there is a legal or professional right or duty to disclose.
Christmas party bill was split in order to get around HMRC tax deductible expense limits.	PROFESSIONAL BEHAVIOUR By asking the Accounts Payable Clerk to breach HMRC rules in relation to the bill for the Christmas party, the director failed to comply with relevant laws and regulations. By failing to confront the director rather than carry out the request, the Accounts Payable Clerk assisted the director in breaching this principle.	The full £160 per head does not qualify as a tax deductible expense and as such should not be treated as one. HMRC rules should be fully complied with at all times.
A director asked a member of staff to produce a set of financial statements that show the company in the 'best possible light' in order to secure a bank loan.	INTEGRITY Producing financial statements designed to mislead the bank as to the position of the company represents a lack of honesty. To comply with the fundamental principle of integrity, a member must be straightforward and honest in all professional and business relationships.	Accounts should be prepared that show a true and fair view of the company's financial performance and position.

Current practice	Principle breached and details	Recommended practice
A director placed an exceptionally large order with a supplier on the basis that the supplier had promised to sponsor a motorcycle show if the order was increased. The director has a favourite group of suppliers, mainly because they are sometimes willing to sponsor his motorbike and racing efforts.	OBJECTIVITY Bias, conflict of interest or undue influence of others should not override professional or business relationships. The director is allowing conflict of interest to affect his professional relationships and judgement. Suppliers should be selected based on the value for money they can offer, not on personal favours offered in exchange for the business.	A formal approved supplier list should be established. Where an approved supplier is not in place, a minimum of three quotes should be obtained and the supplier that offers the best value for money should be chosen.

BPP
LEARNING MEDIA

Appendix 5 – Sustainability review of the accounting system

Sustainability issue	Observation	Recommendations
Corporate social responsibility/ environmental	CCC's mission statement states that 'we are trying to be a greener company and we recycle wherever possible; we promise to remove all of the packaging from customers' premises, and dispose this in an environmentally friendly way'.	This mission statement should be supported by a series of objectives, policies and procedures to ensure this happens in practice.
Environmental	Used ink cartridges are placed in the bin when they are removed from the printer.	These items may need to be disposed of in a specific way due to the chemicals involved. Many types of ink cartridge can be recycled. This should be done if possible.

BPP LEARNING MEDIA

BPP LEARNING MEDIA

Glossary of terms

It is useful to be familiar with interchangeable terminology including IFRS and UK GAAP (generally accepted accounting principles).

Below is a short list of the most important terms you are likely to use or come across, together with their international and UK equivalents.

UK term	International term
Profit and loss account	**Statement of profit or loss (or statement of profit or loss and other comprehensive income)**
Turnover or Sales	Revenue or Sales Revenue
Operating profit	Profit from operations
Reducing balance depreciation	Diminishing balance depreciation
Depreciation/depreciation expense(s)	Depreciation charge(s)
Balance sheet	**Statement of financial position**
Fixed assets	Non-current assets
Net book value	Carrying amount
Tangible assets	Property, plant and equipment
Stocks	Inventories
Trade debtors or Debtors	Trade receivables
Prepayments	Other receivables
Debtors and prepayments	Trade and other receivables
Cash at bank and in hand	Cash and cash equivalents
Long-term liabilities	Non-current liabilities
Trade creditors or creditors	Trade payables
Accruals	Other payables
Creditors and accruals	Trade and other payables
Capital and reserves	Equity (limited companies)
Profit and loss balance	Retained earnings
Cash flow statement	**Statement of cash flows**

Accountants often have a tendency to use several phrases to describe the same thing! Some of these are listed below:

Different terms for the same thing
Nominal ledger, main ledger or general ledger
Subsidiary ledgers, memorandum ledgers
Subsidiary (sales) ledger, sales ledger
Subsidiary (purchases) ledger, purchases ledger

BPP
LEARNING MEDIA

Index

A

Accounting function, 26
Accounting policies, 15, 33, **34**
Accounting standards, 14
Accounting system, **52**, 72
Accounting transactions, 26
Accounts payable (purchase ledger), 26
Accounts payable (purchase ledger) system, 124
Accounts receivable (sales ledger), 26
Application controls, 92, 110

B

Budgetary control report, **36**
Budgeting, 26

C

Centralised, 53
Centralised organisations, 9
Charities, 6
Companies Act 2006, 14
Control activities, 86, **90**, 110
Control environment, 86, **87**, 110
Controlling, 40
Controls, 54
Cooperatives, 6
Cost Benefit Analysis, 143
Costing, 26

D

Data protection law, 15
Decentralised organisation, 10
Decentralised, 53
Decision making,
    Information for, 40
Due care, 65

E

Ethical values, **63**, 72
Ethics, **63**, 72

F

Financial accounting, **29**, 45
Fraud, 118
Fundamental principles, 63

G

General IT controls, 93

I

Industry regulations, 15
    Information for, 40

Intangible, 144
Integrity, 64
Internal audit, 93
Internal control, 54, 86, 93
Internal controls, **86**
IT controls, 93, 110

L

Late payment law, 15
Legislative regulations, 15

M

Management accounting, **35**
Misappropriation of assets, 118
Mission statement, **7**
Misstatement of the financial statements, 118

O

Objective, **3**
Objectivity, 64
Operational information, 40, 42
Opportunity cost, 146
Outsourcing, 29

P

Payroll, 26
Payroll system, 125
Performance measurement, 40
PEST analysis, 61
Physical controls, 121
Planning, 40
Primary objectives, 3
Private limited company, 5
Private sector, 4
Professional behaviour, 66
Professional competence, 65
Public limited company, 5
Public sector, 5

BPP
LEARNING MEDIA

BPP
LEARNING MEDIA

BPP
LEARNING MEDIA

BPP
LEARNING MEDIA

BPP
LEARNING MEDIA

BPP
LEARNING MEDIA

BPP
LEARNING MEDIA

BPP
LEARNING MEDIA

REVIEW FORM

How have you used this Course Book?
(Tick one box only)

☐ Self study

☐ On a course_____

☐ Other _____

Why did you decide to purchase this Course Book? *(Tick one box only)*

☐ Have used BPP materials in the past

☐ Recommendation by friend/colleague

☐ Recommendation by a college lecturer

☐ Saw advertising

☐ Other _____

During the past six months do you recall seeing/receiving either of the following?
(Tick as many boxes as are relevant)

☐ Our advertisement in Accounting Technician

☐ Our Publishing Catalogue

Which (if any) aspects of our advertising do you think are useful?
(Tick as many boxes as are relevant)

☐ Prices and publication dates of new editions

☐ Information on Course Book content

☐ Details of our free online offering

☐ None of the above

Your ratings, comments and suggestions would be appreciated on the following areas of this Course Book.

	Very useful	Useful	Not useful
Chapter overviews	☐	☐	☐
Introductory section	☐	☐	☐
Quality of explanations	☐	☐	☐
Illustrations	☐	☐	☐
Chapter activities	☐	☐	☐
Test your learning	☐	☐	☐
Keywords	☐	☐	☐

	Excellent	Good	Adequate	Poor
Overall opinion of this Course Book	☐	☐	☐	☐

Do you intend to continue using BPP products?   ☐ Yes ☐ No

Please note any further comments and suggestions/errors on the reverse of this page and return it to: Nisar Ahmed, AAT Head of Programme, BPP Learning Media Ltd, FREEPOST, London, W12 8AA.

Alternatively, the Head of Programme of this edition can be emailed at: nisarahmed@bpp.com

REVIEW FORM (continued)

TELL US WHAT YOU THINK

Please note any further comments and suggestions/errors below